THE STORYTELLING ALMANAC

A Weekly Guide to Telling a Better Story

BY

JOHN BUCHER

SIDESHOW
MEDIA GROUP
sideshowmediagroup.com
Los Angeles

SIDESHOW MEDIA GROUP
LOS ANGELES

Printed in USA

Much of the work here appeared in various forms at LA-Screenwriter.com. Deep thanks to Angela Bourassa for providing the opportunity to first share this work.

HOW TO USE THIS ALMANAC

Almanacs have been used for years as annual publications to offer current information about one or multiple subjects. The origin of the word is debated though most likely it is derived from a Greek word, often translated as *calendar*. The most cited almanac remains *The Farmer's Almanac*. Used by farmers to plan for the movements of the sun and moon, hours of low and high tides, rituals and festivals, and various other topics. The end goal was to produce a successful crop at the end of the season. This book has a similar purpose for storytellers -- to produce a successful story.

Suggested Approaches

This book is designed in such a fashion that it can be used in a variety of ways. It acts as a Swiss Army Knife for storytellers. Here are a few ways that you might find it to be a helpful tool.

The Weekly Approach

A conventional approach to this book would be use it as a

weekly guide for improving your storytelling over the course of a year. You will notice that there are 52 short essays in the book, intended to strengthen your storytelling. Some storytellers may enjoy taking on one essay and exercise per week. Creators that choose this method will find a bonus section on seasons and another bonus section on pitching, after the weekly essays have been completed.

The Focused Approach

Some readers may choose to browse the table of contents and take on only the essays that look most interesting to them, ignoring the weekly guide completely. This can also be a helpful approach when using this book.

The Straight Through Approach

Still other readers may find it helpful to read the essays in the Almanac straight through and then return to the exercises they believe will be of most help to them. This may be the most helpful approach for many readers and completely unhelpful to others.

There is not a wrong away to approach this guide. The thinking behind its design is intended to accommodate any approach that a reader may bring to it. In essence, the framework of the book is crafted to trust *you*, the reader, as an expert on what best works for you, as a storyteller.

CONTENTS

WEEK 1

CREATING A PLAN FOR COMPLETING YOUR STORY IN THE NEW YEAR

January brings a season for new beginnings, rededication to lost disciplines, and an opportunity to exercise experiments that can become habits. Many storytellers use the new year as a starting place for birthing a new work. Most writers need structure in order to complete their story in a reasonable time. Putting together a strategic plan for crafting a project is the first step in making what has previously just been an idea in your head a reality. Here are concrete steps you can take in order to complete a new storytelling project this year.

CREATE A SCHEDULE/CALENDAR

Once you've determined the various stages that you will need for your own workflow, you can begin to work on a schedule for each stage. Remember, it's much easier to remove stages that you decide you don't need than it is to have to go back and add a stage that you left out, thinking you wouldn't need it. Determining a regular time each day or each week to work on your project is crucial for most storytellers. Finding a time when you can be alone, concentrate, and be free from distractions is often the greatest challenge a storyteller can face. Early morning, before phone calls begin and people begin to feel others are accessible, can be an excellent time to work.

Your internal editor is not fully awake yet and you may find a greater flow of creativity. Storytellers who make a pact with themselves not to open e-mail, social media, or news sites have even greater chances of success in maintaining a steady work pattern. While some can maintain the discipline of using a digital calendar to schedule their work sessions, others benefit from having a physical calendar hanging on the wall to look at daily, reminding them of their writing schedule and upcoming deadlines. Having a written reminder in front of you constantly can have a powerful effect.

CREATE DEADLINES

Most people acknowledge that they work to completion more often when there is a hard deadline looming. Storytellers are no different. Self-imposed deadlines can be difficult for some to honor. However, publicly announcing a deadline can create a sense of healthy pressure that may allow you to finish a project that you might otherwise let slide. While deadlines should be realistic, they should also be challenging. If the only deadline you set for yourself is to finish a project by the year's end, there will be little motivation to move forward until it's too late. This is why each leg of progress on your checklist should also have an accompanying deadline. Storytellers who have completed the first four sections of a checklist are more likely to be motivated to complete the final six. There is a sense of momentum that helps slow and steady progress feel like a collection of small victories leading to the winning of a larger war. If you miss a deadline, give yourself a new deadline within 3-5 days of the deadline you missed. Don't let one misstep derail your entire process. There are chemical reactors in the brain that reward us when we meet deadlines. The more deadlines we have in a project, and thus meet, the more rewards we will feel in our progress, and the closer we will move towards the finish line.

INVITE A CREATIVE PARTNER INTO YOUR PROCESS

Storytelling can be a lonely business. Having someone to travel the journey alongside of us can make all the difference. Many are reluctant to ask another creator to hold them accountable to monitor progress and deadlines, for a variety of reasons. If you know another willing creator, providing such an offer might be a helpful service to trade. Your creative partner doesn't necessarily need to be a creator working in the same field as you are or a creative person at all. Any close friend can make for a good candidate when drafting someone to hold you accountable for your deadlines and progress. Giving that person a copy of your checklist, schedule, or calendar can make the project more real. Sincerely asking them to check up with you on deadlines and serve as someone to turn your work over to is of greater benefit than relying on the honor system. Selecting someone who you know will consider your request with thoroughness is important. Make sure your creative partner is someone you care about disappointing. While sitting down to create is a solitary act, storytellers can wisely create communities of support around themselves. Remember that those who finish projects are people just like you. They are people who get busy, get distracted, and feel like giving up sometimes. But most importantly, they are people that simply show up consistently until a project is complete.

CREATE A CHECKLIST EXERCISE

One of the biggest mistakes that storytellers make is letting their excitement about beginning a new project drive them into the process without any real planning. Ask yourself how well this method has served you in the past. Do you often finish the projects that you begin this way? Most of us do not. Taking a day or two to plan out the project can make all the difference in whether your new story matures into adulthood or gets stuck in permanent infancy. The first step in planning your strategy is to put together a checklist for the various stages needed to arrive at a final draft. Here are a few things to consider putting on your checklist:

- **Main Character** (Who is this story about? Whose story will I tell?)

- **Goal** (What does this character want? Can this goal be photographed if I'm working in a visual medium?)

- **Conflict** (What or preferably *who* is standing in the way of my character reaching this goal?)

- **Logline** (my story in one sentence)

- **Theme** (What is the one lesson in my story? What is the simple idea my story is about?)

- **Outline** (3-page summary of story – 1 page for each act – beginning, middle, and end)

- **Treatment** (My story in paragraph form – 5 to 10 pages)

- **Detailed Outline** (A brief description of each scene in the story that may include some dialogue)

- **First Draft** (A draft that just gets the entire story with dialogue on the page)

- **Drafts 2, 3, 4, 5...** (Drafts needed to craft the story and work out problems)

- **Final Draft**

WEEK 2

FINDING THE FAMILY OF STORIES THAT YOU SHOULD BE WORKING IN

Ask any story guru, and they will tell you that *very* few storytellers ever develop the skills to master multiple genres. In recent years, however, finding your niche has become trickier as the traditional genres such as drama, comedy, and horror are often combined into hybrids with other genres to create entirely new families of stories. While it might be tempting to write whatever type of material strikes your fancy when you sit down to the computer, learning what works within a family of stories can help you hone your skills and get better at your craft. A number of story experts have suggested new genres that you can explore if that approach is helpful to you. For example, Blake Snyder's "Monster in the House" genre, found in his book *Save the Cat*, encompasses scripts from *Panic Room* to *Jaws* to *Saw*. Finding a family of stories to work in may be helpful if you are wishing to avoid a specific beat structure associated with a certain type of story, as a family of stories has more to do with the emotional core of the story than its structure. Here are a couple of ways to explore finding the family of stories you should be working in.

Check Your Stubs

What films do you care enough about to actually go to the theaters for? In an age of streaming services, one must really want to see a film in order to leave the comforts of home waiting for it to hit Netflix. Sometimes, it's just because we want to be part of the cultural conversation, but often when we actually spend money to go and see a film as soon as it comes out, it's a clue that film may belong in our family of stories. Saving your movie stubs can be an easy way to learn a lot about your own story interests. Getting to know more about who we are as writers will always be helpful in crafting the type of work we aspire to.

Get Out and Explore

So many writers think they know what their family of stories are but have not exposed themselves to enough different types of storytelling to really be sure. While we all enjoy watching the same "comfort" movies we always seem to go back to, getting outside of our comfort zone can expose us to films and TV shows we might not usually encounter. *The Florida Project* is a story I wouldn't have sought out when I first began writing. However, a friend invited me to see an independent film a few years into my work that showed me how stories that revolve around children in tough situations could also have a great deal to say to adults. These stories have slowly morphed into my family. You might be surprised how exposing yourself to new types of stories can keep your work fresh and constantly evolving and expanding.

Finding Your Themes Exercise

Make a list of twenty of your favorite films, even if you plan to tell a story in a different medium. Go back and try to determine the big themes in each film. Did it deal with the theme of returning home? Fathers and sons? Appreciating what you have? After having listed the themes you remember for each film, begin looking for patterns. Are there themes that appear again and again? Are some themes similar to others? Try to find three key themes that are *your* themes. These may be the themes that you should be writing about, as they are clues to your values and worldview.

WEEK 3

PREPPING FOR A NEW STORY

If you are serious about beginning a new story, this is the perfect time to start preparing so that you can actually get down to the business of writing. Here are several ways to start seriously preparing to complete a new story this year.

RESEARCH

How much do you know about the world you want to set your story in? Research is important for almost any project, but it's especially important if your story is a period piece or takes place in a world that you have not lived in yourself. This may include another geographic culture, another lifestyle such as the world of doctors who work in hospitals, or a subculture such as the worlds of drugs or criminals. Even if you are setting your story in a world familiar to you, you should consider researching the occupation or leisure activities of key characters in your story. If your protagonist is an elementary school teacher and you have never held such a position, knowing the challenges and realities of someone who has becomes important in making the story feel authentic. Your research may only need to be brief or it may require more extensive dedication but making sure you truly understand the world your story takes place in as well as the people that inhabit that world is essential for making the writing process flow smoothly.

CHOOSE A PROTAGONIST

Granted not *every* story revolves around the journey of a *single* character, but many do, and even if your story will be the exception, it's not a bad way to begin branching into the other characters in the narrative. Really getting to know your character before trying to tell a story about her will greatly assist you in the decisions you will later have to make on the character's behalf. One method of getting to know your protagonist is writing 3-5 pages of backstory about the character during your story preparation time. Even if little or none of the history you create for the character ever gets used in the final draft, knowing who that character is and why she makes those decisions not only makes plotting the story easier, but will also make the character feel more human when executed on the page. Another helpful exercise can be writing a few pages about what your protagonist's day was like the day before the story you are telling begins. Even the simple minutiae of the character's life can make her feel more real as we begin taking her through a journey that will resonate will audiences.

CHOOSING AN EXTERNAL GOAL

Getting into a character's internal journey is often the place many writers gravitate towards first. While this is an essential piece of the character, without an external goal, our character may quickly meander about and become boring to the audience. Internal journeys are hard for audiences to see unless they are revealed through external desires. Knowing what your character wants gives he or she purpose in the story. Revealing why they want it is important as well but may well come later in the writing process. Determining the visual elements of your story, such as the external goal, is a good way to give the narrative a skeleton that flesh can be put on throughout the rest of the writing process.

CREATING AN OUTLINE EXERCISE

Not every writer creates an outline before beginning the storytelling process. However, far more writers *should* be creating an outline beforehand than actually do. The excitement of writing can motivate us to completely skip the less "sexy" parts of the process, even though outlining is completely for our own benefit. Outlining helps writers work through story problems and logic issues before trying to execute subtext and dialogue. Few writers ever regret taking the time to work their story completely through in an outline. Remember, outlines don't lock us in from creativity. They actually free us to be creative with other aspects of our story once the structure is in place. We don't decorate our skeletons and organs, but our flesh is adorned with clothes, makeup, tattoos and even scars and bruises. This is only possible once we have the bones to hold up the flesh everyone will be looking at on first glance.

Create a one-page outline for your story with the major moments that you want to see happen as the story plays out. It may be helpful to create three "buckets" to put these moments in – a beginning, a middle, and an end.

WEEK 4

HOW TO BEGIN A NEW STORY

At the beginning of the year, many storytellers are launching into their latest ideas and reviving old ones. One of the most difficult hurdles to overcome, when beginning a new story, can be the opening. Where do you start? What does the audience need to know immediately and what can be revealed over time? What will be engaging and what will be confusing? In our age of short attention spans, we only have a few minutes to capture the imagination of someone who is giving our story a chance. What are the most effective means of using that precious time? Here are a few ways to hook your audience just as your story is launching.

THE CHARACTER HOOK

Opening with the lead character is almost always a solid way to begin a story. It psychologically communicates to the audience whose story this is and who we should care the most about. Whenever stories open with a different character, rather than the protagonist, there is always a risk that the audience will be confused and have to recalibrate once the protagonist is introduced. *Three Billboards Outside Ebbing, Missouri* opens with Mildred Hayes, the lead character in the story who immediately piques our curiosity with her sudden interest in three dilapidated billboards on the edge of town. *The Marvelous*

Mrs. Maisel opens in a similar fashion with our heroine standing before a live audience telling jokes. Both stories tell us who the protagonist is while simultaneously causing us to wonder what is motivating her to do what we see her doing.

THE INTRIGUING MOMENT

Whether or not a story opens with the protagonist, making the first on-screen moments interesting is essential. Giving the audience an unusual situation, scenario, or action can build interest not just in what is being witnessed, but also in who the characters involved are. *Lady Bird* opens with the protagonist and her mother together in bed, inside a cheap motel. We are invited to consider the nature of these two women's relationship and whether they were forced to share a bed or chose to. When it is established that this is a mother and her daughter, it only peels back layers of more questions rather than simply answering our initial inquiries. *The Florida Project* opens with young Dicky yelling to his friends, Moonee and Scooty, that there are "freshies at The Future." Even though it is Moonee that will emerge as the protagonist, the moment itself is intriguing, as we are immediately curious as to what "freshies at The Future" are and why these children are so excited about this discovery.

THE BACKSTORY

With some narratives, it is most effective to establish the events that will lead to the moment that will send the protagonist out on her or his journey. While building backstory seems like a natural entry point for every story, caution must be exercised, as audiences may not later recall the details of these important events later, since they do not have a frame of reference for who the characters are. The most helpful backstories build organically and develop the narrative as well as the character at the same time. In *The Disaster Artist*, we are given a quick introduction to the passion, desires, and absurdity of Tommy Wiseau, while also establishing how he met Greg Sestero. Their relationship is not only necessary to launch the story but also serves as the ever-evolving core, around which all the events which will follow happen. *Downsizing* provides the backstory for how the world where the story takes place became possible in its opening scenes, without yet revealing the protagonist we will follow.

ESTABLISHING THE WORLD

A certain amount of world building must be done in the early stages of every story. However, wisely choosing the events and visuals of the opening scene can craft the narrative in such an efficient way that the audience feels initiated into the world of the story before they have met any of the significant characters or know any plot elements. *Dunkirk* opens with paper leaflets falling from the sky, which we quickly see are propaganda. Not only is this interesting visually, it also sets up the world where this story takes place very quickly. Each episode of *Black Mirror* deliberately gives the audience clues as to the world of the story before unfolding the central conflict that will play out.

BEGINNING WITH THE ENDING

While not always the right approach, sometimes letting the audience in on how the story resolves and then going back to reveal how the events led to this moment draws the audience's attention and interest in trying to piece together the narrative. This "bookending" approach is a classic trope of storytelling that continues to remain powerful, even as storytellers find unique ways to execute it. In *I, Tonya*, the story begins with seeing the present state of all the characters involved. We see the humor and tragedy of their lives, and are then curious as to what led to the embittered relationships that we now see. In the opening moments of *The Shape of Water*, we see a woman, we will come to know as our protagonist, sleeping underwater. How is this possible? How did she get here? What led to this unusual situation? We are looking forward to the events of the story before we even know what they are – which is exactly the frame of mind the storyteller hopes to put an audience in.

BEGINNING A NEW STORY EXERCISE

Brainstorm three different ways to open the story you are writing or thinking of writing. For each opening, write down what emotions you want the audience to feel in during this scene. What about the scene will hook the audience, causing them to want to know more?

WEEK 5

STORY CHECK LIST

There are certainly no formulas to creating a good story. None that work anyways. There are, however, forms. Good music uses chords that resonate together. Painting uses color systems that work in unity or intentional disunity. Photography uses composition techniques to most effectively draw the eye through the story of the image. The list goes on. Sometimes, we complete a story that works really well in some areas yet falls flat in others. It seems unbelievable that we could craft a story and somehow forget something significant – until it happens. While every story is different, here's a checklist of elements your story might be missing and desperately need in order to generate effective storytelling.

1. A Protagonist Or Protagonistic Force

This seems like a no-brainer. It's hard to imagine a good story without at least one character in it that we relate to and root for. Yet, dozens of pitches are given every day about a concept that never mention a specific character in the story. Concepts are great, but people connect with *characters*. Many new creators get so excited about the idea they have for their story that they end up constructing shallow flat characters that no one will care about. Make sure your story has a protagonist or group of protagonists, not just a main character. A protagonist is someone we understand on some level, even when we can't agree with them. A protagonist is a character that we enjoy watching and rooting for (or against). A protagonist is someone we become invested in as the story plays out. But perhaps most importantly, a protagonist is someone we see ourselves in.

2. An Antagonistic Force

Even if there's not a specific person who serves in the role of the antagonist, there should be an antagonistic force. Otherwise, we will have no conflict, which we will discuss in a moment. For some reason, many writers fight like mad to keep a separate human antagonist character out of their stories. Sure, stories where the character is battling against something within themselves can be interesting. But we need to *see* something with our mind's eye in most modern stories. This is especially true if you are working in a visual medium. Watching someone battle inner conflicts or demons exclusively is pretty boring in a film, unless you are Terrence Malick or someone of his ilk, and let's face it, most of us are not. Antagonistic forces can take the form of a weather phenomenon such as a tornado, an institution such as a prison system, or even a shark that fights the town for control of their beach – but whatever form the force takes, it needs to be there. New storytellers should consider sticking to external human antagonists before entering the tricky waters of internal antagonists or other more nuanced forces.

3. An External Goal

Without an external goal for your protagonist, your story can meander about. What is actually going to *happen* in this story? Thinking and talking can be fascinating in real life. However, people rarely remain interested in stories that feature those activities exclusively. A good place to begin in determining your protagonist's external goal is asking yourself what they want and what they will do to get it. The higher the stakes for reaching their goal, the better the story. Finally, remember the external goal is just that – external. We need to be able to take a picture of it if you are working in a visual medium. A woman trying to find love or acceptance is interesting, but you can't take a picture of that and have an audience understand what they are seeing. Goals such as those are also difficult because we have trouble understanding when they have been accomplished. How do we know when she finds love? We *can* take a picture, however, of a girl who finds a date to the prom. Remember, the more specific and photographable the goal, the more the audience will relate to it in visual stories.

4. An Internal Goal

You might know *what* you want your character to accomplish in your story, but do you know *why*? Many times, the more general external goal we first formulate is actually a better internal goal – see the example about finding love above. The internal goal does not have to be photographable, so more abstract and internal processes are acceptable. Gaining respect, learning to be a better person, and overcoming selfishness are all excellent internal goals. The internal goal should be learned through the process of achieving the external goal. We enjoy seeing external goals in stories, but internal goals are *why* people engage them.

5. Conflict

At their heart, stories are about characters dealing with and overcoming conflict. We all have it. We all relate to it. We want to see characters find ways to reconcile theirs. It's reassuring to us. If that person I love in that story I love can find a way around the things that are causing them pain, maybe I can as well. If your story is missing significant conflict, people won't likely care. Indifference is the enemy of the storyteller. Cause some trouble for your characters. Create some conflict.

CREATING CONFLICT EXERCISE

Brainstorm three terrible things that could happen to the protagonist in your story. Describe the details of how horribly this will impact the character. If you have trouble coming up with ideas, think about what happened on the worst day of your character's life.

WEEK 6

HOW TO CREATE A WORLD FOR YOUR STORY

There are a number of ways that a storyteller can begin crafting their story. Many begin with a character – the protagonist. Others begin with a concept. While there is not one "right" way to begin constructing a story, there are many ways to help jumpstart the process. One such method is to begin by creating the world that your story will take place in. When putting the world of your story together, it can be quite tempting to begin inserting characters, especially a main character that will traverse this world. While this isn't always a bad thing, it can be a healthy discipline to remain focused solely on the world and not allow yourself to specify a character just yet. Here are a few steps to creating a world for your story without immediately bringing a character into the narrative.

CREATE A CULTURE

At first, the thought of creating an entire culture for a world may seem overwhelming. It's not necessary to take an academic approach to the task, detailing every aspect imaginable. Look for two or three major characteristics that will define the culture. Even one single description can paint a vivid image of the culture of the world. For example, we might describe a culture by saying this is a world where spells and magic

---

still exists. Or we might describe the world, saying it's a place where slavery is commonplace and freedom is rare. Whatever our description, we are trying to get down to what makes the place unique or different from the world we know – even if the story will take place in our world. We might describe the culture in *Game of Thrones* by saying it is a world where noble families fight for control of mythical lands. Switching the approach to a culture we might find in our modern world; a cultural setting could be described as the high-stakes dating world within Black community of Los Angeles – as is the case with *Insecure*.

CREATE VALUES

The values of the people within a given world tell us a great deal about its inhabitants. If life is cheap, we more thoroughly understand the landscape a protagonist must navigate in order to accomplish her or his goal. If acquiring and keeping wealth is the highest value of the world, we expect the story we create will likely deal with themes of greed, betrayal, and perhaps even extortion. In *Toy Story*, being played with is a value within the culture of the toys. Turning to a completely different world, power is the ultimate value in *The Deuce*. Establishing what the people within the subculture of your story hold dear not only gives the audience insight into the characters you will later introduce, it also opens up plot possibilities for the story. When a value is threatened or violated within a culture, we will naturally expect conflict – the driving force behind any story.

CREATE A CONCEPT

Sometimes, the concept for a good story is the first thing we think of. However, as part of creating a world for our story, building a simple conceptual framework for the narrative is a helpful part of the process. To be clear, the concept for the dynamics of the world may be quite different than the concept of the specific story you create. While they may be similar or even exactly the same, the concept of the world often has to do with the issues within the world that lead to conflict -- which we will look at in more detail in a moment. One way to approach the concept within the world is to begin with the question, "What would happen if...?" What would happen if cars transformed into human-like beings with personalities? What would happen if there was a spiritual battle between knights with martial arts skills in outer space? What would happen if a UFO accidentally left one of its crew members on earth? The concept should be simple and easy to understand. Details can come later. With *Breaking Bad*, the concept behind the story doesn't even bring drugs or power into the equation. It modestly asks, what happens when people find out they have cancer and will die leaving their families with nothing?

CREATE CONFLICT

Knowing the central conflicts in the world of a story help us understand the stakes and the pressures that the characters in that world deal with. When we know the culture, values, and concept of a world, the conflict can become obvious. For example, if our story world is one where wealth and tradition trump emotions, where the highest value is marrying within your class, we can guess that the conflict might involve star-crossed lovers from opposing tribes. As stated earlier, the conflict should rise as a result of a transgression of values. In the world of *A Simple Favor*, being a good parent is the highest value. When that value is transgressed, conflict spins out of control. The level of conflict that arises tells us a great deal about how important the lapsed value was within the world of the story, which in turn makes the world feel more authentic to the human experience – a value all storytellers should care about.

CREATING A WORLD EXERCISE

Write a single paragraph describing the world your story will take place in. Remember, the goal is not to describe every detail but to instead provide details that help the audience understand the "rules" and "feel" of the world.

WEEK 7

APPROACHES TO SETUPS AND PAYOFFS

One of the most vital yet least discussed aspects of effective storytelling is the ability to execute potent setups and payoffs. While it may seem like common sense, the demonstration of this skill is often the factor that separates amateur stories from effective ones. Setups and payoffs don't just happen in a story. They require planning. They often require rewriting, in order to properly associate the setup and payoff. While a setup can involve a mere mention of something or an inferred question early on in the narrative, a masterful setup will have deeper thematic significance than simply referencing an unimportant detail. It will take on greater meaning when the payoff is revealed. In the same way, a powerful payoff will open up the story, or a character, in a new and sometimes unexpected way. Here are a few approaches to crafting setups and payoffs that will make them feel emotionally resonate to your audience.

ALIGNING THE SETUP AND PAYOFF

One of the most common mistakes in executing setups and payoffs is misalignment, where what is set up is never paid off or what is paid off was never properly set up. When misalignment occurs, its usually because the storyteller failed to complete enough drafts of the story to catch the misalignment and fix it or because she or he hasn't yet developed the skill of identifying the misalignment. While this skill comes with time, recognizing good setups and payoffs in other stories can be a helpful way of beginning to identify how to make them work in your own story. In *Crazy Rich Asians*, we learn that the protagonist, Rachel Chu, is a professor of game theory. While it may seem like a trivial detail, this setup is paid off near the end of the story when her occupation becomes meaningful in helping her skillfully confront her antagonist. If Rachel had used the game of Mahjong in overcoming her enemy without any explanation, we would have been left asking why she had such expertise in the game and was able to use it to her advantage. In essence, we would have had a payoff that was not setup.

AVOIDING THE DISAPPOINTING PAYOFF

Even when we recognize that we have a setup that should be paid off, it can be difficult to create a payoff that has the punch we know the audience will be expecting. When first learning how to create relationships between setups and payoffs, we may struggle with creating a payoff that feels emotionally satisfying. One way to begin sharpening this skill is to create lists of possible payoffs for a particular setup. What are all the ways that this setup *could* be resolved? Often, we simply spend all our time focused on finding the one perfect solution, rather than looking for a variety of options to choose from. When we create a menu of possibilities, new ideas may unexpectedly arise. In *Coco*, the writers lead us to believe that Miguel's grandfather may actually be the great singer, Ernesto de la Cruz – an intriguing setup. The payoff could have confirmed that this was true. It could have also been simply that this wasn't true, after Ernesto's true character was revealed. However, the writers chose to instead go with a completely different option

WEEK 7: Approaches To Setups And Payoffs

than what the most obvious payoffs would have been – to make the man who had been there for Miguel throughout the story his real grandfather, a surprise the audience doesn't see coming, though somehow, we feel we should have. Not only do the writers execute a payoff that clearly took several drafts to come up with, they manage to add irony to their choice, as Miguel's real grandfather, Hector, is initially presented as a trickster without much interest or ability to help Miguel, which leads us to our final approach to setups and payoffs.

MASTERING THE IRONIC PAYOFF

While eventually answering a question that we pose early on in our story will bring the audience satisfaction, it may or may not be emotionally powerful. Irony can involve a protagonist getting what they need but not what they want, or vice versa. It may also involve the answer to a plaguing question coming from an unlikely source. It can also involve the protagonist not being able to use what they think will solve a problem and being forced to rely on something completely unexpected. In *Operation Finale*, protagonist Peter Malkin anticipates it will be his desire for revenge that will be useful in bringing antagonist Adolph Eichmann to justice. However, in the end, it is his humanity that makes the task possible – an unexpected and ironic payoff for a commanding setup.

SETUP AND PAYOFF EXERCISE

Brainstorm three setups and payoffs for the story that you have been crafting or one you've been thinking about creating. Remember to try to include an element of irony in your payoff.

WEEK 8

APPROACHES TO BETTER DIALGOUE

Even of the most masterful storytellers and talented executors of plot can cause their narratives to grind to a screeching halt when their dialogue strikes an audience as unnatural. It's a common misconception that creating dialogue is simply about mastering the way people speak to each other in real life. Our conversations contain nuance and local colloquialisms that work well at the neighborhood watering hole but don't necessarily draw the reader into the internal and external journeys of the characters on the page. The way dialogue is most effective in a story greatly depends on the medium. In scripts for film and television, dialogue can be its own art form, but must give each character their own unique voice. Here are approaches to dialogue that will bring the audience deeper into the story, rather than taking them out.

KEEP IT SHORT

One of the most common mistakes new storytellers make is having their characters explain the plot of the story to each other through dialogue. Occasionally, even experienced storytellers fall into this trap. If you are working in a visual medium, the story should be told through the juxtaposition of images, only using dialogue to enhance the visual narrative the audience is seeing. If long blocks of exposition are required, there may be a better medium for the story. After an initial draft, storytellers would do well to go through every line of dialogue and ask themselves if it is absolutely necessary and what it gains the audience in experiencing the story. Being a hard editor on the words the characters will speak can help you keep sections of dialogue short. Short words, short sentences, and short exchanges are effective in having your audience stay focused on the unfolding plot and who the characters really are, rather than being distracted by unnecessary talking. Certainly, there are exceptions to this principle, and a number of successful creators who have built careers by *not* doing this but leaning into concise dialogue usually serves developing storytellers best.

BECOME A LISTENER

Get out of your head. For some creators, this can be a tough thing to do. While listening to the exact way people talk might not necessarily work for crafting dialogue, as mentioned above, listening to what people talk about, how they make small talk, and the way they use language to relate to the person they are talking to can be extremely helpful. Observing people is a good practice for a storyteller to get into anyway. Listening to people talk helps to create organic interactions between the characters you create. It's an old adage, but it's true – most of the time we are waiting for our turn to speak rather than truly listening. While it's easier to observe when we listen to the conversations of others, paying close attention to our own conversations and the emotions we experience as we speak, as well as when we speak without really thinking, can be insightful when creating similar interactions for our own characters.

STUDY SUBTEXT

Eventually, seasoned storytellers recognize that what is not being said in a scene can be just as powerful as what is given voice. The underlying subtext can give a scene tension, make it humorous, or deeply moving. The small talk a couple makes around the breakfast table as they prepare to discuss custody of their children may appear benign if we only look at the words being spoken. However, the inner angst we know the characters are experiencing can give those words much more meaning and gravitas. Asking what the character speaking is *really* trying to say, what they *really* want, and what they are afraid of letting show can be a good starting point for crafting dialogue that has substance beyond the content of their words. Creating subtext is a skill that takes time to master, but an effort well worth the undertaking. Linda Seger's *Writing Subtext: What Lies Beneath* is an excellent tool for learning more about what subtext is and how to create it. While not every scene needs subtext, knowing which scenes do and how to get the most from those scenes can mean the difference between a master of the craft and a novice.

CRAFTING DIALOGUE EXERCISE

Brainstorm three scenes that demonstrate a child hinting to a parent about what they would like as a birthday present, without just explicitly saying it. Try crafting one of the scenes with no dialogue at all.

WEEK 9

WAYS YOUR CHARACTER CAN DEMONSTRATE WHAT (OR WHO) THEY LOVE

Demonstrating internal processes inside characters can be difficult. Seeing that a protagonist has learned a lesson, realized their greatest fault, or found true love can be challenging to paint with an external brush, since these transformations happen inside a character's psyche. Showing an audience what your character truly loves can provide a window into who they really are. Here are ways your character can demonstrate what he or she loves.

ACTIONS – What They Do

While words are quite important, as we will discuss, they are not enough for love to feel genuine. We need to *see* and *feel* someone's love through their actions. Sometimes the most subtle gesture can move emotional ice bergs. Other times, a gargantuan expression of love is required for the action to feel authentic. The appropriate actions a character must take to show love is unique to that character. It can be revealed to the audience through backstory, through early moments in the narrative, or through dialogue from others in that character's life. The actions a character takes should cost them something, as we will discuss momentarily in the section on sacrifice.

Denzel Washington gives a powerful monologue about the actions he performs out of love for his son in *Fences*. However, Washington's actions seem benign when the young man never hears his father *tell* him he loves him. In *Moonlight*, we see Black travel to a diner to see Kevin late one night and *feel* the love he still has for this character. Casey Affleck's character has great trouble telling his nephew how much he loves him in *Manchester By the Sea*. However, the entire film's actions serve as a love letter from one character to another.

WORDS - What They Say

Love is expressed in a wide variety of ways across cultures. However, studies have shown that if someone never expresses their love to us verbally, we have serious doubts about whether they love us at all. We have an innate need to hear the words. Our characters can demonstrate their love for people, places, and things, but there may very well be moments in your script that the audience needs to hear that character articulate their feelings. Of course, this is risky, because articulating such intimate feelings can come across as cheesy. It's also tempting to have a character simply state their feelings and then never have him or her back up those words with actions, leaving the expression feeling empty. Writing dialogue when expressing our most intimate of human experiences can be tough, but can also be one of the most powerful moments in your story. Take a look at Sandra Bullock's heartbreaking words about her family in *Gravity*, Ben Affleck's epic love confession in *Chasing Amy*, and Tom Cruise's tearful bedside speech in *Magnolia* for excellent examples of characters expressing their love through words.

TIME - Where They Spend Their Days

We can learn a lot about who or what someone loves by tracking how they spend their time. We tend to give time to those we care the most about. We usually spend our free moments doing those things we enjoy the most. Our characters are no different. We see Theodore's love for Samantha in the amount of time he spends with her in *Her*. We see Bliss's love for roller derby through the amount of time she dedicates to practice, competition, and emergence in the culture of the sport in *Whip It*. We see Martin Luther King Jr.'s love for the people of his community through the time he dedicates to their progress in *Selma*.

SACRIFICE - What Are They Willing to Give Up

Perhaps the most powerful expression of love in both stories and real life is when we witness what a character is willing to give up for a person or a cause they believe in. Sacrifice is one of the most commanding indicators of love in every culture. There is a certain dramatic irony in asking a character to give up something they love for someone else. An important principle is that we only ask characters to give up something that costs them. Otherwise, the stakes are not raised through the character's sacrifice and the audience fails to fully invest in the moment. Audiences most love seeing a character give up something that they may have had to give up themselves in their own life. In *12 Years a Slave*, we see Solomon sacrifice his pride, his ego, and even his body for his wife. In *The Iron Giant*, we see the beloved protagonist lay down his life for the people he has come to care about. Jim Carey's character gives a powerful speech about sacrificial love in the comedic *Bruce Almighty*. Of course, sometimes sacrifice can be seen through a negative lens. Watching a character sacrifice their family for drugs or alcohol can also be heartbreaking. People sacrifice for the people, places, and things they care the most about. Our characters must do the same.

SHOWING LOVE EXERCISE

Write two to three paragraphs about a time when the protagonist in the story you are working on (or have been thinking of working on) expressed love to someone. How did they go about it? Was it difficult for them? What were the results or consequences?

WEEK 10

THE CONFLICTED PROTAGONIST: APPROACHING FLAWED CHARACTERS

As often as we all strive for perfection, we rarely appreciate it when we see it in others – including characters in stories. The woman that never has a bad day, the co-worker that's never in a bad mood, and the man who hits the lottery every time he plays all suffer from the same narrative disease. They are all annoying and quickly become boring. Ironically, many of us create characters plagued with the same disease. While flat characters that serve a single narrative purpose have their place in stories, protagonists, antagonists, and significant supporting characters are far more compelling when they are multi-layered, which means they have flaws as well as likeable qualities. Where does one draw the line, however? Can a character's flaws actually cause them to cross the line into unlikability? Are there actions she or he can take that the audience will never forgive over the course of the story? This can vary from viewer to viewer. Some viewers have sensitivities to character conflicts involving any sort of abuse, mistreating children, discrimination, and heteronormative behavior. While few characters will hold appeal for every audience member, here are a few approaches to giving your characters flaws that decrease the chances of alienating your audience in the process.

My Own Worst Enemy

Audiences' sensitivities usually revolve around how a character treats others. Most audiences have a great deal of empathy for characters that function as their own worst enemies. This is likely because we have all fallen victim to self-inflicted mistakes. In other words, we can relate. While this approach may involve the character making decisions that do end up affecting others negatively, the wound inflicted by the character should impact that character most significantly, especially if that wound is internal. Jack's alcoholism in *A Star is Born* affects those in his sphere, but no one loses more than he does as a result of his behavior. In a completely different genre, Bruce learns that he has been blind to the fact that he is actually more responsible for his problems than anyone in the comedy classic, *Bruce Almighty*. In *Widows*, Veronica comes to terms with the fact that turning a blind eye to her husband's dark side has now turned her into her own worst enemy, who must be defeated before she can face the external enemies after her.

The Kind-Hearted Killer with a Code

We tend to give lots of grace to people who make horrible mistakes if we view them as kind people. Establishing that a character is kind before showing the ugly underbelly of their personality can go a long way in keeping the audience on board for their journey. A number of stories, such as *Dexter*, have made audiences empathetic towards those who commit the worst imaginable behavior, when we see that they are kind to or protective of children, the weak, or the vulnerable. Seeing that someone is not *all* bad, can be as important as establishing that they are not all good either. Even when we see a character commit awful offenses, we psychologically rationalize it if we like the character and have established that their actions are a part of some code of ethics. Mike Ehrmantraut kills a character we greatly empathize with in *Better Call Saul*, but because we have established Mike's compassion and care for his granddaughter and the difficulty he undergoes when carrying out the actions of the code he has chosen to live by, we still support him as a character.

The Self-Aware, Sacrificing, Sinner

Those who seem unaware of their own selfishness and bad behavior often strike us as the worst to interact with. Unless coming to a sense of self-awareness will be a key element in your character's arc, those who lack recognition for those around them are difficult for the audience to connect with. However, we tend to go a long way with those who are aware of their own shortcomings. Issa makes decisions that hurt those she is in relationship with in *Insecure*, but we constantly root for her to learn from these decisions because she is so quick to own up to her mistakes. Those who can muster up the strength to apologize for when they fall prey to their worst inclinations garner even more favor with audiences. We can attribute this to the fact that audiences enjoy seeing characters that represent the best of who we would like to be. Characters with faults in one area can make up for in, in the audience's mind, by sacrificing in some other area. This communicates an understanding of our own experiences when we are forced to navigate the nuanced decisions we are constantly faced with in life. We are usually moved by seeing sacrifice, especially when that sacrifice involves a character's own pride. In *Beautiful Boy*, David must finally admit his own powerlessness to help his son. Only then can he complete the archetypal journey his character is on, and actually empower his son to fight his own dragons.

FLAWED CHARACTER EXERCISE

Write a paragraph for each flaw the protagonist in the story you are creating (or have thought about creating) has. Describe the ways those flaws have impacted the character as well as others.

WEEK 11

WAYS TO ENCOUNTER "THE OTHER" IN YOUR STORY

Some of the most impactful themes in storytelling revolve around an encounter with "The Other." Often representing something else than what is obvious, "Others" are what we fear, what we are curious about, and what we long to understand. When "The Other" is the protagonist, our story often falls in the "fish out of water" genre. However, "Others" can be used in storytelling in a wide variety of ways. *The X-Files* made a weekly habit of searching for "Others." *Orange Is the New Black* explores the idea in subtle ways. *Suicide Squad* places "The Others" as the heroes of the tale. The *X-Men* franchise is completely built around the concept. "The Other" can come in many forms. Giants, aliens, monsters, and strangers have all suddenly appeared on our narrative horizon, bearing lessons for us as "The Other." Here are ways to use and explore the concept in your own story.

"The Other" as Friend

Many stories begin with "The Other" frightening us, only later to become a friend. When audiences first encountered *E.T.*, he seemed far from cute and cuddly. It's only through the journey of the film that we begin to care about him and his mission. Eventually, the alien becomes our protagonist's best friend.

He is loyal and kind, but still unlike us. He reminds us that we often fear things that later become familiar and helpful to us. The same lessons and themes are apparent in Steven Spielberg's movie, *The BFG*. *Tarzan* begins as "The Other," then becomes "one of us" only to be forced to return to his role as "The Other." His connection to nature and the wild reminds us that "The Other" can come in forms not *completely* foreign, but still unfamiliar. Tarzan is unconventional, alien to us in many ways, yet still connected to us in deep and perhaps even unconscious ways. The title of the story alone assures us that *Dr. Strange* will be "The Other," yet we will still root for him. In *Me Before You*, Will Traynor is "The Other" in Lou Clark's world. He eventually becomes her friend and then lover.

"The Other" as Foe

There are stories that begin with "The Other" frightening us but never transition into them being anything friendlier. *The Shallows*, *The Conjuring*, and *The Walking Dead* all act as shining examples. *Ghostbusters* uses unfriendly "Others" to comic effect. The aliens in *Independence Day* are very different than aliens like E.T. They also begin with a frightening presence but never stop embodying such through the remainder of the story. Presenting "The Other" as foe can be a slippery slope thematically. It's easy to reinforce our human tendencies that cause us to be afraid of those different from us. It also can be subtlety communicated that those who are different are evil and should be destroyed. It becomes important to try to stress the idea that it's not what makes us different that should be eliminated, but rather our fear, prejudice, and hesitancy that might cause us not to confront evil head on. This can be done in a variety of ways. One of the most common is to demonstrate that "The Other" strikes first – that they have malicious intent toward us and plan to eradicate us if we don't stop them first. Our willingness to fight should come as a last resort and should only be in response to evil deeds, in order for our story to resonate with the better judgement of civil society.

Fables are an old form of storytelling that were used to present "The Other" as foe. Most people are familiar with fables such as *The Tortoise and The Hare.* What few in our culture recognize is that these tales were never meant to characterize one person as being like a tortoise and another like a hare. Instead, they communicated that inside of *all of us* is both a tortoise and a hare. We should try to emulate within ourselves the tortoise and avoid the temptations of the hare. In other words, fables taught us to confront "The Other" inside ourselves -- to battle against our inner "Others" that weren't helpful in our journey. For it is these "Others" that we all face as foes.

"The Other" as the Unseen Numinous

Sometimes, "The Other" isn't embodied at all in a story. Sometimes, it represents an unseen force that might take positive or negative forms. In the case of the *Star Wars* saga, the "Unseen Numinous" is literally called *The Force.* No one ever sees it. Obi Wan Kenobi tells us that it surrounds us and even flows through us. It represents the transcendent – the divine – that which we cannot control. In these sorts of stories, "The Other" is not something we try to make friend or foe, but instead something we align with or try to join in some form of understanding. Indiana Jones often must meet the "Unseen Numinous." In *Raiders of the Lost Ark,* we see angels *and* demons unleashed when the Ark of the Covenant is opened. They are "The Other." The numinous is briefly seen, but those who do keep their eyes open to see, are quickly destroyed. "The

Other" as the Unseen Numinous can also been seen inside of us. Some stories that take on a deep inner journey tackle this idea.

Whatever "The Other" is in our story, we should treat it as an opportunity to present the audience with a challenge. "Others" may be within us or very much a part of our actual existence. Regardless, the truths and metaphors remain the same. Facing "The Others" in our own paths and either learning to befriend them, fight them, destroy them, or make peace with them is a worthy goal for any story.

THE OTHER EXERCISE

Brainstorm two different forces that might represent "The Other" in your story. How will the key characters in your story respond to "The Other"? How will "The Other respond to them?

WEEK 12

BURDENS THAT CHARACTERS MUST BEAR

Fleshing out characters can be a complex and tedious task. Deciding what details open up who the character is for the audience and what is simply minutiae takes maturity that usually only comes with practice and the development of skills. One of the key insights for crafting characters that feel real is determining what weighs on their mind as they go about their day – their burdens. These burdens can be parsed in a variety of ways, depending on the story you are telling, how obvious these burdens are to other characters, and if the burdens become central to the plot or remain motivational factors in the character's psyche. Here are three basic categories of burdens that will help you craft characters that are universal, relatable, and emotionally resonate for audiences.

Regret for What They Did or Didn't Do

The weight that many of us carry around often centers on regret. Some of us regret the things we've done. Others regret those opportunities we never had the courage to take. Whatever the source for our regret, a scar remains, reminding us of what might have been, if only we made different decisions. Decisions are what lie at the heart of regret. When the audience knows that a character has either exercised bad judgement or made mistakes in the past, we gain insights into what patterns of behavior the character struggles with and may be prone to do again. Similarly, if a character missed an opportunity to have something she wanted, but couldn't bring herself to commit to, we gain insights into what lesson she may have to demonstrate she's learned later in the narrative. In *Widows*, the regret that Victoria experiences for turning a blind eye to her husband's criminal involvement, drives her toward her own criminal pursuits. Nancy Eamons experiences a very similar type of regret in *Boy Erased*, having stood by quietly as others made decisions about her son's life.

Guilt or Shame for What They've Done

Researcher and author Brené Brown has said that guilt results from what we have *done* but shame results from who we *are.* This is an important distinction to remember when crafting characters as it speaks to the character's feelings about their experiences and if they have internalized those feelings as part of their own identity. A character may feel regret for what he has done because he got caught but might not experience any guilt or shame for the action. A character might also feel guilt for something he's done, but not regret it or feel any shame about it. Additionally, a character may feel shame about who they are though he has done nothing regrettable. The ways that we distinguish between guilt, shame, and regret give the audience nuanced understandings about the complexity of a character's humanity – which is important in making the character feel real. Freddie Mercury experiences shame about who he is in *Bohemian Rhapsody*. His battle with shame and the pain it causes in his life drives his artistic expression and creates a uniqueness in how he approaches music, which in turn serves as a balm for his agony. Gary Hart's character in

The Front Runner appears to regret what he's done when he sees how it affects his family but doesn't seem to experience any guilt about his actions or shame for who he is.

Responsibility For Others

Some burdens are not about the character at all but involve the weight brought about by the character's relationship with someone else. Most often that character is someone in the protagonist's family, as is the case in all the examples below. The weight the character experiences can involve feeling responsible for another character's death, as is the case with Neil Armstrong in *First Man* and Clara in *The Nutcracker and the Four Realms*. It can involve a character the protagonist couldn't save, as is the case with Lisbeth Salander in *The Girl in the Spider's Web*. Or it may involve the responsibility a protagonist feels in protecting another character's legacy, as is the case with Adonis Creed in *Creed II*. Feeling responsible for someone other than ourselves is near universal in the human experience. Most of us have another person in our lives that we would be willing to sacrifice for and take on burdens to protect. Knowing who your protagonist feels this way about connects her or him to the audience, making us willing to shoulder the character's burdens as well.

THE CHARACTER'S BURDEN EXERCISE

Write two to three paragraphs about the burdens that the protagonist in your story (or a story you have been thinking of creating) bears.

WEEK 13

PROTAGONISTS WE DON'T SEE ENOUGH

We have a difficult problem in the storytelling world. Creators are told to write what they know. However, most writers that have historically broken through to bring their stories to larger audiences are white males. In turn, we have had an overwhelming number of stories about them and their culture. Of course, the answer to this problem is to empower more creators who do not identify as white males into the market. Does this mean, however, that writers should only create lead characters that match their own gender identity and ethnicity? Few would see that as the path toward the best storytelling environment either. There have been numerous examples of films where a writer has co-opted someone else's story for great profit and in turn, made a mess of that story, because the writer did not truly understand the culture or characters from that world. There are a variety of ways to approach stories from outside of what we know, however. Research and interviews from within the culture the story occurs is a good starting place. Working on the story with a co-writer from within that culture or gender identity is another strong approach. And of course, if you are a writer that resonates with the ethnicity or gender identity of your protagonist, let this serve as an encouragement for how badly we need to hear your stories. While there are a wide variety of roadblocks and pitfalls, there are a number of protagonists we don't see enough of in storytelling. Here are a few of them.

PROFESSIONAL PEOPLE OF COLOR

The TV landscape has improved in the past few years with shows like ABC's *Scandal* and HBO's *Insecure* but the film world has been slower to embrace people of color in professional roles as protagonists. Athletes, entertainers, and crime figures have all been archetypes that minorities regularly are cast as, but rarely doctors, lawyers, and teachers. Asian and Indian actors are even more rare in these roles than their African American colleagues and of course, men far outnumber women in these positions as well. The world is full of men *and* women from every ethnicity serving in professional roles. More stories would do well to reflect this, especially with their protagonists.

PARENTS AND GRANDPARENTS

It's no secret that our world has a fascination with youthfulness. Stories about parenthood are often only used as b-stories that complicate the protagonist's life, making what they *really* want to do more difficult or humorous. Being a parent is a key part of someone's identity. Seeing mothers and fathers in new and fresh contexts remains a rarely tapped field of opportunity. Grandparents get even less time in stories, usually being relegated to tired stereotypes. Even when older actors are centrally featured in a story, it is often to show how they too are youthful. Exceptions do exist and are welcome changes of pace. The film *Victoria and Abdul* is a positive example from director Stephen Frears, the filmmaker that has made a career of telling stories of parents and grandparents, including *The*

Queen and *Philomena*.

PEOPLE OF FAITH

An overwhelming number of people in the world claim belief in a power higher than themselves. However, religious faith is often seen as a weakness in a character or the butt of a joke. While supporting characters in *Grey's Anatomy* and *The Leftovers* have been vocal about their faith, protagonists that believe are often harder to find. Granted, the faith community has an entire genre where *every* protagonist is a person of faith. However, these films are often poorly told stories that are only meant to exist in a small bubble of Christianity. A wide array of faiths exist in the world, yet protagonists seem to reflect so few of them, especially in stories centered in the United States.

WOMEN WHOSE SEXUALITY OR RELATIONSHIP DOES NOT OVERLY DEFINE THEM

The conversation around the sexualization of women in storytelling has been going on for decades. Progress has been made but the discussion has become even more nuanced and complex as subjective ideas about how these issues are defined and executed fill the spectrum. Sexuality is an important part of who we are. Stories that explore this should be welcome. However, the paths that lead to exploitation and debasement are many. Even when sexuality is not explicitly in focus, heteronormative stories where a woman's relationship to a man is often what defines her in many narratives. The progress that we have experienced in this area can be somewhat attributed to female storytellers finally getting to tell their own stories. However, male storytellers are not then free to ignore building wholeness into characters simply because women have now been invited into the conversation. Moving stories forward into deeper realms of beauty and truth is the responsibility of everyone.

THE RARE PROTAGONIST EXERCISE

Create three protagonists that you've never seen in a story before. Write a paragraph describing each one.

WEEK 14

STEPS FOR MAKING PECULIAR CHARACTERS BELIEVABLE

Stories rely on the strength of their characters. The more memorable they are – the better. However, if we, as an audience, don't buy the characters, we quickly lose interest in whatever their goals or struggles are. Crafting characters that feel real can be tricky for a number of reasons. In an effort to make our characters feel authentic, we sometimes base their characteristics or backstories on people we know in real life. While this can be an effective method, sometimes, life is actually more unbelievable than fiction. Scores of writers have justified odd plot twists in their stories, insisting that this is really what happened in the life of someone they know. Audiences are willing to suspend a certain amount of disbelief when engaging a character, but there's a thin line that can be difficult to maneuver. Most of us enjoy a quirky character living as the fish out of water. However, peculiar characters can easily become annoying to audiences when we begin to doubt their believability. Here are steps for creating characters that your audience will love, regardless of their idiosyncrasies.

GIVE THEM STRONG MOTIVATION

There's perhaps no greater factor in persuading us to believe in the authenticity of a character than strong motivation. When we identify with *why* someone is the way they are or do what they do, we will saddle up next to her for any journey. *Lady Bird* is desperately trying to escape her small town and trivial life. We begin to understand *why* as her story progresses – she doesn't want to become her mother. This universal theme regarding the complexities between parents and children dates back to at least Oedipus. We innately understand children not wanting to become their parents, despite the strong love they may feel for them. A twist on this theme often occurs when a character is orphaned or when their mother is missing from the story. There is a strong but subconscious motivation to connect with the world and fill the gap left by the missing parent, though the character is usually extremely bad at it. *Juno*, *Napoleon Dynamite*, and *Superstar* are all examples of these types of stories, featuring eccentric but believable characters with strong motivations.

MAKE THEM SINCERE

Sincere characters are hard not to love. Sarcasm, bitterness, and insecurity has made sincerity a true act of vulnerability in our culture. When we see it, we are intrigued, wishing we might could embody more of this genuineness ourselves. In *GLOW*, Ruth Wilder is a character filled with nuance and layers. She also remains sincere throughout her journey, causing us to love her more deeply, as an audience. When she suffers injustice, sexism, and is the recipient of other's vitriol, she never becomes resentful or a cynic. This doesn't mean that we never see her emotional, crushed by sadness, or even tempted to give up. It simply means that her resolve and sincerity acts as a north star to which she always returns. *Trainwreck*, *The Big Lebowski*, and *About A Boy* all center on sincere but individualistic characters that we can laugh with, but secretly want to *be like* in some way. Their sincerity causes us to believe them and believe *in* them.

PROVIDE US DETAILS

It's the little things that often cause us to believe. The small details about what a character likes, their habits, and even insecurities can be fascinating when they serve to reveal to us who she or he is. The character of Annie in *Hereditary* is an artist that creates miniatures. Ari Aster, who wrote the script, could have simply alluded to the fact that the character is an artist. However, the details regarding the type of art she creates provide us not only with insights into who she is and how she views the world but also become useful in developing the plot of the story. *Oceans 8*, *Solo: A Star Wars Story*, and *First Reformed* all offer levels of detail about their characters that make want to invest in their journeys. The way a character dresses, what they eat, the car they drive, and what part of town they live in can all be useful details in making them believable. The key temptation to avoid is providing details about a character that do not seemingly have any meaning or offer any insight into who the character is.

GIVE THE AUDIENCE A VOICE

The final step in making a character believable has little to do with the character in question at all, but instead depends on the development of *another* character in the story – the voice of the audience. When a character has an unusual way of moving through their world, it is important that someone else in the story be aware of this and point it out. This is psychologically reassuring to the audience that the feelings they may be having about the character are valid. This recognition gives the audience permission to connect with the character regardless of any red flags their foibles may raise. In *Deadpool,* the character Weasel will often voice what the audience may be thinking of Wade Wilson. The audience enjoys laughing at Weasel's clever banter with Wilson as it mirrors the perceptions they have been feeling about the protagonist of the story as well. Drax serves this role in the *Guardians of the Galaxy* franchise. Shuri offers a similar voice in *Black Panther.* The character that gives voice to the audience often does so in a humorous way but also in a way that keeps the protagonist's ego in check. They can remind the hero where they came from and keep them from the traps of narcissism. When the audience's feelings and concerns about a character are given voice, the individual they are asked to follow becomes much more believable.

THE UNBELIEVABLE EXERCISE

Create a new character for this exercise. Write a single paragraph describing who this character is and what they want (their external goal). Then write a second paragraph that describes *why* they want this – their motivation.

WEEK 15

WAYS TO APPROACH DESIRE IN YOUR MAIN CHARACTER

One of the most compelling ways to move your protagonist through every scene in your story is to keep his or her desires just below the surface in the subtext. Clueing the audience in to what the character *really* wants in each scene makes for rich interactions that keep your dialogue from being squarely on the nose. Of course, before we can subtly communicate the desires of our character to the audience, we have to fully understand those desires ourselves. While it can be tempting to create a character that is unable to identify exactly what she wants, because we are also trying to figure this out as the storyteller, we as creators must know precisely what the character desires before we can construct a believable journey of self-discovery. Here are ways to approach crafting desire in the psychology of your character.

DESIRE FOR THE MATERIAL

External goals are essential for most stories. They identify to the audience what the protagonist is trying to accomplish in the story. They also conveniently let the audience know when the story is over, as the protagonist will either accomplish or not accomplish that goal. When we can see what the main character desires, it should be easy for the audience to also recognize the prize. Material desires can include everything from wealth to buried treasure to a simple watch with great sentimental value. It is rarely the object itself that carries the value (though it can be) but more often what the object *means* to the character. A poor street kid may attempt a grand heist to possess the valuables inside a museum, but it's how those valuables will allow that kid to change his life that mean the most to him. Endowing the material with greater meaning is the key to compelling desire for the material. In *Bad Times at the El Royale*, Dock O'Kelly desires a bag of hidden money. Discovering that his brother died while hiding the money for him makes his search for the cash more enthralling, however.

DESIRE FOR THE INTERNAL

While the material drives many characters into conflict pursuing their goal, even more characters' desire what cannot be seen – what exists deep inside themselves. Internal desires can be tricky to execute without relying on exposition. However, skilled storytellers learn to develop methods for communicating the deepest desires of a character's heart, without she or he ever having to articulate those wants. Sometimes the internal desire is for self-forgiveness. Other times it is to accept who the character truly is. Still, other times it is to overcome the insecurities that have made it impossible to receive the love of another. Finding peace and meaning after the death of his daughter seems to be what Neil Armstrong desires in *First Man*.

DESIRE FOR CONNECTION

The answer a character is looking for may well be inside her – but not always. Connection with another person, a group of peers, or even society as a whole may be the driving force of desire your character experiences in the narrative journey.

The desire for connection is a universal human archetype. We *need* other people. Some need lots of other people and some need only a few. However, we are all bound by the fact that human beings do not do well alone for long periods of time. The most common connective desire is, of course, love. Crafting a character that is shaped like a puzzle piece can be a challenging task. A protagonist's quirks, peccadillos, and misjudgments can make us squirm when crafting them. But when we introduce a character whose own puzzle piece is shaped to fit exactly along the curves of the protagonist, it is a rewarding experience for the writer and the audience alike. Midge is in many ways an awkwardly shaped puzzle piece in *The Marvelous Mrs. Maisel*. Watching her attempt to connect with her parents, Susie, and the rotating group of men that come in and out of her life can be humorous. When we see her experience true connection in the story, however, it becomes hard not to feel the same emotions her character is experiencing onscreen.

DESIRE FOR CHANGE

What a character desires is often rooted in what will benefit him. Some characters instead desire what will help their family, their community, or society as a whole. A desire for change in systems and institutions can mirror the journey a character experiences when he desires change within himself. That desire may also look different. Many times, some sort of sacrifice will be required in order for the protagonist to affect change. This sacrifice is often ironic as it usually involves some person, object, or ideal that the character *also* desires. Forcing a character to make a difficult choice between two things they want makes for engaging storytelling. The audience cannot help but ask themselves what they would choose in such situations. In *Veep*, Selina Meyers desires change in the bureaucracy of the federal government. That change often humorously comes at the cost of her own dignity.

APPROACHING DESIRE EXERCISE

Select a character from a story you are creating or have been thinking of creating. Write one paragraph about what that character's desire is. Then write a second paragraph about what how far the character is willing to go for that desire.

WEEK 16

STUCK IN THE MIDDLE: WAYS TO UNTANGLE THE SECOND ACT OF YOUR STORY

This is specifically for storytellers crafting work with a beginning, middle, and end – using the classic three-act structure approach. However, even if you are not presently or have not ever designed a story with this framework, you may still find this discussion helpful. The first act of a story is often the most fun to write. You get to build worlds, construct characters as well as their backstories, and set up the conflicts and troubles that await your protagonist. The end of the story can also be exciting to craft. The final showdown you've waited the entire story to unleash, the redemption you've been waiting to have your character experience, and the killer monologue your character gets to voice are just a few of the elements that might await you once you've closed the book on the first two acts of your story. Gurus have offered a number of different ideas about how the second act can be created. Michael Hague has suggested it be sliced into two separate acts. Blake Snyder offered a number of different beats that could occur during the window including the fun and games, midpoint, and dark night of the soul. The possibilities can be endless. While there's certainly no formula to what makes a strong second act, there are a number of different methods to untangling the story when it seems to be going nowhere or even worse – feels stuck. Here are ways that might propel things into forward movement.

THE REVEALED REVERSAL

Reversals are powerful tools that can be used at a number of different points in your story. However, the second act is a prime location to issue a revelation to your protagonist that will result in a change of plans or fortunes. It may or may not affect the external goal that your character is chasing but it should definitely affect how she gets goes about achieving it. In *Mad Max: Fury Road*, Furiosa spends the first half of the story trying to get to the Green Place. When she does finally arrive, near the midpoint of the story, it is no longer there. The reversal results in a change of plans and a new goal for her and her team. In *Get Out*, Chris Washington learns that the parents of his girlfriend are not really the people they claimed to be. His goal shifts from getting closer to them to getting away from them. In *Logan*, it is revealed that Eden, the place our hero has been tasked with delivering a little girl to, is actually part of a comic book tale. The revelation cleverly leads to an even greater reveal in the third act.

THE UNEXPECTED OPPORTUNITY

Some people love surprises. Others hate them. Regardless of how your protagonist feels about them, they are a part of life, and often a part of good storytelling. Dropping something unexpected in your character's lap, during the second act, can be a way of taking the plot in an unexpected direction. Mia is offered the chance of a lifetime in the second act of *La La Land*. Ironically, the opportunity may cost her what she has come to love most. In *Moonlight*, Chiron is invited to act on the feelings he has had for a lifetime. The opportunity also comes at great cost for him. The third act results of his opportunity turn out much different than they do for Mia, but life is forever changed by the opportunity given to both characters in this crucial section of the story. In both, *Room* and *Green Room*, our protagonists are given unexpected opportunities to escape the prisons they have found themselves in. Again, the results of these opportunities vary greatly in each story. For some characters, it leads to a better life, and for others it results in death.

GOING ALL IN

The second act of your story often allows the protagonist to go "all in" on the tentative decision they may have made early in the story to involve themselves in what turns out to the be the plot. Seeing a protagonist put themselves at greater risk, physically or emotionally, usually causes a greater level of empathy in the mind of the audience. In *Manchester By the Sea*, Lee Chandler is thrown into caring for his nephew, Patrick. Over the course of the second act, we see him truly embrace the situation, and actually *decide* to care for the boy. In *Arrival*, Louise Banks is given the opportunity to decipher the language of an alien species. In the second act, the task takes on a greater emotional resonance and drives her to greater success. Conor dyes his hair and stands up to the bully that has made his life hell throughout the first half of *Sing Street*. This commitment to his art and a different life symbolizes the heights that he is now been motivated to. Similarly, in *Lion*, Saroo takes his questions about his family of origin to new planes of commitment in the second act. He goes "all in" to find them.

THE PREPARATION

Sometimes, our protagonists must learn life lessons and go through preparation for the final challenge that awaits them at the end of the story. These moments can make for a powerful second act. They may experience formalized training, difficult defeats, or near-misses at what they crave. What becomes key is that the protagonist changes and develops over the course of the experiences. In *Rogue One*, Jyn is gifted with the necessary team and skills she needs to accomplish her mission at the film's conclusion. A less-than-perfect singer trains her heart out for the concert of a lifetime in the second act of *Florence Foster Jenkins*. She never achieves perfection but does accomplish powerful triumphs along the way. In *Hacksaw Ridge*, Desmond Doss must stand his ground in the trials of the second act, so that he can take the ultimate stand required in the third. The preparation a character receives makes all the difference in the believability of their victory in the finale.

SECOND ACT EXERCISE

Identify three to five stories that have first acts similar to the story you are creating or a story you've created in the past. Then identify the major moments in the second act of those three to five stories. Consider what you have identified as a beginning point for outlining possibilities for your send act.

WEEK 17

ANIMALS AS SYMBOLS FOR STORYTELLING

The relationship that we have with animals is unlike any other. Some animals we love and invite into our homes as family. Other animals we revile and imagine as pure evil. The most ancient stories that humankind told often involved animals, as they offered kinship, antagonistic struggle, and sources of food in areas where plants and vegetables didn't easily grow. Aside from the characters they have embodied in storytelling, animals have long carried mythological symbolism as well. While readers and viewers might not be fully aware of the meaning behind an animal's use, thinkers from Carl Jung to Joseph Campbell have suggested that their symbolic implications speak to us in unconscious ways. Animals do not even have to serve as actual characters in a story to communicate themes and ideas. A protagonist can sit on a park bench and simply see an animal. The presence of that animal in the story can suggest what the character is thinking or what will soon happen to her. In *Rampage*, Dwayne Johnson deals with three different animals that have become infected with a dangerous pathogen. Each has a different meaning for Johnson's character. While the animals in your story might not play as big of a role as the gorilla in *Rampage*, there are subtle ways to involve non-human creatures in the themes and plot of your narrative.

Here are four animals that can be used in multiple ways as symbols in stories.

BIRDS

Though birds carry many unique qualities, none has quite captured the human imagination as powerfully as their capacity for flight. Birds can represent a character's potential to escape their circumstances. They can symbolize our striving for the transcendent heavens. They have the ability to carry numerous meanings for us, depending on their shape and color. Alfred Hitchcock used them to symbolize mysterious evil in *The Birds* and explicit evil in *Psycho*. J.K. Rowling used them as the symbol of freedom to help Albus Dumbledore escape in *Harry Potter and the Order of the Phoenix*. Rowling used birds in several of the Potter stories to symbolize a vast array of different meanings. Crows and ravens have long symbolized the ominous, the evil, and even death itself. Vultures have similar impact. Doves have symbolized Aphrodite, angelic presence, and the concepts of peace, hope, and promise. And of course, we are all familiar with the wisdom symbolized by owls, the majesty of falcons and eagles, and the insights of the peacock, with the many "seeing eyes" on its feathers.

RATS and MICE

In *Ratatouille*, Remy the rat chef states, "I'm a rat, which means life is hard." Filmmaker, Noah Baumbach offered a different perspective in a story he penned for the New Yorker called *Mouse au Vin*, saying, "Mice are so weird. They're like humans in rodent costumes." Like birds, rats can symbolize a wide scope of things -- everything from struggle to human beings, themselves. These creatures can strike fear in those that encounter them or serve as their pets. The ability of mice to squeeze their bodies through small places speaks to the tenacity they offer as symbols. In *The Departed*, Jack Nicholson's character gives a memorable monologue about the disgusting nature of rats, warning those around him not to betray him. However, in Hindu mythology, rats are often companions and helpers, as they also are in *Cinderella*. *Stuart Little* and *Mickey Mouse* have both embodied mice as symbols of innocence and the adorable. *An American Tale* uses mice to symbolize the very human feeling of being an outcast. With the ability to represent the best of ourselves and our most grotesque fears, rats and mice offer a great number of narrative possibilities.

DOGS

There are few creatures in the animal kingdom as beloved as the dog. While Wes Anderson's *Isle of Dogs* has stirred controversy for its use of racial motifs and potentially appropriated culture, few can argue with the themes used in the film around what dogs mean to those that love them. Films such as *Old Yeller* and *Where the Red Fern Grows* carry deep meaning for many because of their relatability to those who have lost dogs as pets. Of course, dogs are not always used in stories as the loyal colleague. Mythological tales about the hounds of hell, and inhabitants of the underworld are just as common as tales of canine nobility. Stephen King's *Cujo* is a noted example of the power of dogs to represent unleashed rage and evil. Despite these portrayals and uses, the loyalty of dogs like *Bolt* and Toto in *The Wizard of Oz* will eternally make dogs symbols of the best of what we hope for in others...and ourselves.

HORSES

Nearly as beloved as dogs, horses have long been used as symbols of strength, endurance, and life's mysterious ability to carry us from one moment to the next. Horses have a special relationship with American storytelling, thanks to their archetypal uses in the earliest Native narratives of this land to the western expansion that was only made possible through their determination. Muybridge's horse has a significant place in the use of film as a storytelling medium. Horses were also integral to the first American film that told a story, *The Great Train Robbery* in 1903. From *The Black Stallion* to *Flicka* to *War Horse*, these graceful animals have served as central figures to the development of protagonists. Horses have symbolized power, mutual bonds and benefits, and freedom in stories. Their mere image in a story brings a psychological environment of open emotions for many viewers. From *Spirit* to *Seabiscuit*, horses remind us of the power we have when our own wildest drives and impulses can be tamed and focused in productive ways.

ANIMAL EXERCISE

Write two to three paragraphs on how you might use animals in a story you are creating now or would like to create. Does the protagonist have a dog? Would certain animals lend themselves to specific types of symbolism in your story?

WEEK 18

Stories Within Stories

Have you ever wondered if they watched movies in the world of *Star Wars*? Or if the superheroes in the Marvel films were aware of DC's Superman and Batman? Some of the most fun moments in *Ready Player One* were seeing characters ranging from Freddy Krueger to the Iron Giant co-exist in the same world, as they do in our own. Seeing the characters in a Steven Spielberg film actually be aware of Spielberg's other movies presented an entertaining existential challenge that worked alongside the larger thematic questions that the film was addressing. Whether we recognize it or not, when we tell stories, we make constant decisions about the relationships between the world of the story we are creating and the real world we live in. Sometimes we avoid mentioning the sorts of details that make characters most like us – the music they listen to, the TV shows they binge watch, and the movies that inspire their lives. Bringing these pop culture products into a script can be problematic, as they can date a story, or isolate an audience that doesn't feel the same resonance with the film or TV show the character loves. Other times, knowing that a character in a film we like also was impacted by a TV show that impacted us can make that character even more resonate for us. Here are questions to consider when including stories inside your own story.

Does it help the audience better understand your character?

Any details we include about a character's preferences should help to reveal who that character is. Knowing that *Tomb Raider*'s Laura Croft likes jelly beans doesn't reveal anything about her psyche, though this writer is pretty confident that would be her snack of choice. However, finding out that Wade Watts has a deep knowledge of the Atari 2600 game, *Adventure*, which was popular decades before he was born, tells us that he pines for something missing in his world. That missing element turns out to be real world connection and becomes significant to the plot.

Does it help the audience better understand the world the characters live in?

Instagram is mentioned and seen throughout the film, *Gemini*. Its inclusion reinforces the image driven, celebrity-crazed world that the protagonist, Jill, lives in. It also becomes a significant tool in solving the mystery at the heart of the story. When pop culture phenomena open up the world of the characters *and* are useful as plot elements, their use feels even more organic. Knowing that *Orange is the New Black* exists in Dominika's world in *Red Sparrow* might be a fun bit of trivia but doesn't really tell us anything about the high stakes domain of espionage that she is a part of.

Does it cause the audience to ask other questions that will be distracting?

While seeing *E.T.* exist in the world of *Ready Player One* is rewarding, we notice that Spielberg was careful not to include *X-Men*. It could be distracting if we remember that Tye Sheridan, who is playing Wade Watts, also played young Cyclops in

X-Men: Apocalypse. Including this, while it might be a fun Easter egg, calls out the philosophical problem of whether this film could exist in the world of *Ready Player One*, since the same actor plays in both. While there could be explanations for this, as storytellers, we don't want the audience drifting off into philosophical considerations instead of staying engaged with the narrative at hand. Walking the line with including other stories inside our own story can be tricky. When done well, the audience is rewarded and further engaged. When distracting, the audience may lose the through line of what is happening in the story *you* are telling and might never return.

STORIES WITHIN STORIES EXERCISE

Write two to three paragraphs about stories that might exist within the world of the story you are creating or one you would like to create. What books has your protagonist read? Do they watch television? What is their favorite show?

WEEK 19

STORY LESSONS FROM SOPHISTICATED WOMEN

The larger storytelling world continues to struggle with representing stories from the many different perspectives found in our ever-changing world. Fortunately, many cinematic stories are beginning to offer narratives through the eyes of one of the most historically underrepresented voices in film – those of women – with more regularity. Women of varying identities, ages, ethnicities, and occupations are being seen on screens around the world, which is cause to celebrate. Of even greater significance is that these women are multidimensional and crafted with layers of complexity. Here are story lessons we can take from the sophisticated women in cinematic stories.

AUTHENTIC CHALLENGES ARE NEVER ABOUT A SINGLE ISSUE

Hidden Figures

Based on the true experiences of Katherine Johnson, Dorothy Vaughan, and Mary Jackson, this story goes beyond the challenges of three women overcoming racial prejudice, which is certainly significant in their journeys. Aside from dealing with the issues that surround the color of their skin, these characters also wrestle with the challenges of being women in the workplace, the struggles of keeping up with the latest technologies, balancing home and work lives, the nuances of romantic relationships, even time management. Combining so many realistic difficulties throughout the paths of these women, makes the characters feel real, true, and human. We watch them intently, hoping to gain insights into the similar issues we face.

INTERESTING OCCUPATIONS SUPPORT INTERESTING STORIES

Arrival

Amy Adams portrayal of Dr. Louise Banks has garnered attention from audiences and critics alike. The genre of Science Fiction has long blazed the trail of placing women in roles traditionally held by men. Sigourney Weaver broke down doors with *Alien* in 1979 that women are still walking through today. Banks is a linguistics professor in the story, a fascinating occupation that uniquely qualifies her to interpret the language of the visiting aliens. When writers build an *interesting* character with an *interesting* occupation, *interesting* stories are usually not far behind.

GOOD BACKSTORY MOTIVATES CHARACTERS

Rogue One

Rogue One's Sergeant Jyn Erso (Eadu) is a highly skilled soldier in the Rebel Alliance. But before we learn anything about her present dilemmas, we learn about why she is motivated to do what she does, the events that made her who she is, and what ghosts haunt her. Learning about the single event that shaped her life as a little girl tells us a great deal about what we can expect her character to do throughout the rest of the story.

We also know what drives her and what she is fighting for. Understanding a character's motivation helps audiences relate and root for her.

PEOPLE ARE OFTEN BUT NOT ALWAYS WHAT WE NEED

Moana

The filmmakers of *Moana* explicitly state in the script that our protagonist in *not* a princess. Disney has previously received criticism about female characters always needing romantic involvement with a male character to complete their journey, usually in the form of a prince. *Moana* breaks that mold. Much of the narrative revolves around the discovery that she does not actually *need* the strong male character, Maui, in order to accomplish her goal. We do see Moana need people in her life, her grandmother for example, but romance is not essential for making her a fully realized person -- a sophisticated lesson for a sophisticated woman.

PERFECTION IS NOT REQUIRED OR DESIRED

20th Century Women

20th Century Women tells the story of three women -- Dorthea, Julie, and Abbie – at different stages of life. It may be the most nuanced portrayal of the journey of women to hit screens in some time. All of the women are far from perfect. We see them make mistakes. We see them experience regret. We see them accept their failures. This does not weaken the women as characters, it actually makes them stronger, because they feel more authentic – more like the women we encounter in our day to day lives. Audiences want to imagine what they could be when they encounter a story. However, the also insist on seeing who they are.

SOPHISTICATED WOMEN EXERCISE

Select one of the films mentioned above that you have NOT seen. Watch it this week and then write two to three paragraphs of reflection about the women centered in the story.

WEEK 20

EXERCISES FOR DEVELOPING THE PSYCHOLOGY OF A CHARACTER

When we create characters, we make choices about who those characters are. Though we may never use the exact term, what we are really doing is creating the psychology of those characters. In other words, we are painting a picture of how their mind works and specifically how that affects their behavior. It's easy to mistakenly make choices about a protagonist's behavior that doesn't quite fit with the psychology that has been established throughout the story. This can cause a character to feel inauthentic. However, when we take the time to deliberately craft out a character's psychology, the chances that we will write behaviors for them that feel false decrease dramatically. Here are five writing exercises for developing the psychology of your character that will not only help *you* get to know *them* better but also help create authenticity in their impulses and behavior.

CREATE A TIMELINE OF THEIR LIFE'S BIG MOMENTS

Identifying the defining moments in our own life helps us understand who we are. These moments are what shape us and offer insight into the motivations we have in matters of love, occupation, and hobbies. You can choose which, if any, of these moments are actually revealed over the course of the story you are telling about the character. However, simply knowing the character's biography and timeline helps us understand who they are internally – their psychology. In *Eighth Grade*, we never find out who or where Kayla's mother is. But we can bet that writer Bo Burnham knows the answer and used it to make her character more authentic and compelling, while simultaneously allowing the audience to feel the absence.

CREATE A FAMILY TREE

Knowing what tribe we descend from can be key to understanding our place in the world. Having some sense of our ancestry tells us about the people and circumstances that brought us into this world. This holds true for a character as well. As with the timeline of their life's big moments, you may choose to reveal little of your protagonist's actual family tree. The entire benefit of creating one will likely be for you as the crafter of the character's psychology. What we can be sure of is that every person and their thinking is somehow shaped by those the people in their family – even if the response to one's relatives is rebelling against them. The degree to which a character's family influences their current life will be different with every story, but can be a useful tool in helping us understand why a character makes the choices they do. Stories ranging from *Knocked Up* to *Wonder Woman* have used family trees to develop the psychology at the center of their narrative.

MAKE LISTS ABOUT THE CHARACTER

Some readers may remember a favorite tome available at their local library called *The Book of Lists*. More than one writer had the flames of their curiosity stoked by this simple idea that supplied seemingly infinite matters of jest and otherwise useless facts. There can be something powerful about creating lists, however. Certain lists can offer us a great deal of understanding into who a person is. In a memorable episode of *The Office*, Michael Scott asks Pam Beasley to make sure his magazine subscriptions are forwarded to his new address. The moment offers a ripe opportunity to list the magazines the character subscribes to. Scott's list not only includes GQ and Maxim, but also Cracked Magazine. The list reveals a great deal about who this character is psychologically. Creating a list of what magazines your character subscribes to, what web sites they have bookmarked, or what podcasts they regularly listen to may help you develop their state of mind in moving through the world, and may also offer an opportunity to bring this useful information into the story you are writing as well.

CREATE A PINTEREST BOARD AS THAT CHARACTER

Making a character's psychology visual is a helpful way to truly *see* who they are. Determining the images that they identify with tells us a great deal about how they think and what they find interesting. As the saying goes, a picture is worth a thousand words. Creating a Pinterest board as though you are your protagonist can get you into their psyche. It's simply one way of seeing the world through their eyes.

WRITE A LETTER AS THAT CHARACTER

We've all heard the bit of advice offered by armchair therapists – write the person that has hurt you a letter, but don't send it. Writing a letter to someone in the voice of your character provides a unique opportunity that we usually don't have when writing a script. We can hear what is going on inside the character in a manner that just doesn't usually happen in screenwriting. You may decide to have your character write a letter to someone who has hurt them or who they are angry with, but don't feel limited to these emotions. Writing a letter to an unrequited love, the teacher that influenced them to choose their career, or an aunt that was always there for them can be equally powerful. Imagine Ethan Hunt, from *Mission Impossible*, writing a fan letter to a hero *he* admires. Like many of the exercises above, this letter will likely not have any place in the actual story you are writing. Remember, the point is getting inside the character's head and better understanding what makes them tick – their psychology.

WEEK 21

SIX CHARACTER PROMPTS TO PRACTICE DEVELOPING BACKSTORY

As storytellers, keeping our tools sharp is a necessary part of the craft. Sometimes, a scenario pops into our head and we rush to create characters to plug in to the story template we've created. However, great stories often come out of well-developed characters. One effective way to create a new story can be to construct the narrative around a fascinating character you've already shaped, as opposed to taking the opposite approach.

Characters with multiple layers and well-developed back stories often share a few common traits. One is a *wound* or a *ghost*. A wound is something that was done to the character before the story begins. It's a scar they cannot stop looking at. While taking part in the external journey they are involved in, they are secretly hoping to bring healing to their wound – even though they might not consciously know that. In *War Dogs*, both main characters have their wound referenced by supporting cast, though they never directly speak to their wounds, themselves. A ghost is a figure from the protagonist's life that still follows him or her around, metaphorically. The shadow of the ghost seems to loom large over everything they do. While this sounds like an ominous situation, it can be found in the most jovial of comedies. On *The Office*, Andy Bernard is constantly trying to escape the ghost of his father, who is still living, but is an omnipresent force in everything Andy says and does. Here are six character prompts you can practice developing backstories around, complete with either the character's wound or ghost. If you're in a hurry, write 1-2 pages of back story for one of these characters. If you have more time, try writing 4-5 pages.

TOMMY GRANADA

Age: 23

Prompt: He is the son of one of the wealthiest tech billionaires in the United States.

Ghost: His mother. Even though he seems destined to follow in the ruthless footsteps of his father, friends and family keep telling him of the kindness and generosity of his deceased mother.

SARAH DIAZ

AGE: 29

Prompt: She has just been elected sheriff of the town she grew up in.

Wound: Her brother was convicted of a crime when she was a child. He was killed in jail. It was later proven that he was innocent of the crime he was convicted of.

AMARA KAPOOR

Age: 42

Prompt: She discovers a fellow professor at the university she teaches at is involved with an underground racist movement.

Wound/Ghost: She was the only person of color at every school she attended in England. One particular bully made her life hell throughout her formative years.

SANDY SOMMERS

Age: 77

Prompt: He has a secret. He's the only gay resident of Sunnyside Nursing Home, but no one knows this.

Wound: The only time in his life he expressed his true feelings for someone, he was rejected and shamed.

SHAQUITA SKARSGARD

AGE: 33

Prompt: She's just married the man of her dreams. Only one challenge in her mind – she's black and he's white. That and no one in her family knows.

Ghost: On his death bed, her grandfather, who was injured in the civil rights movement, asked her to never marry outside her race.

RAYMOND ENGLISH

Age: 17

Prompt: He's in love with the single mom next door. They seem perfect for each other, except….it's illegal obviously.

Wound/Ghost: His mother died giving birth to him. Could this be psychologically intertwined in his feelings for his neighbor?

WEEK 22

THE NUMBERS GAME: 3 CONSIDERATIONS FOR AGING YOUR MAIN CHARACTER

None of us are getting any younger. Fortunately for us, our characters can effortlessly move through time to whatever age we deem most helpful for our stories. There have been successful projects featuring people of every major age demographic, so what should we consider when assigning an age range to our protagonist? Here are some key considerations for how many candles to put on your main character's birthday cake.

CONSIDERING EXPERIENCE

Remember when you were learning to drive? You were face to face with fear, excitement, and power. However, the experience probably taught you nothing about the complex and nuanced ways that romantic relationships worked. Some things only come through living life, not through simple achievements. Our scars, our war stories, our pain, and our laughter make us who we are. If an audience is to feel empathy for your character, they must believe that character is real. Characters only feel real when they seem to have had the appropriate life experiences that would inform the scenario they find themselves in. Most teenagers will not understand the complicated range of emotions one experiences watching their friends die regularly – at least not in the same way that someone in their 80s would. Similarly, someone in their 50s will likely have had too many life experiences to know the passion of a first love in the way that a 14-year-old might. The experiences that a character has had can also link to the genre of the story that you are telling. Many comedies have been based around a character ironically *not* having the appropriate experience in a situation. Morgan Freeman, Michael Caine, and Alan Arkin become octogenarian bank robbers in *Going in Style*. Steve Carrell was a *40 Year Old Virgin*. Robert De Niro's character was re-entering the work force in *The Intern*. Rigorously working through a protagonist's backstory before you ever begin crafting your story can help you flesh out the truth about the life a character has lived before we meet them.

CONSIDERING TIMESPAN

Determining how much your character will age over the span of the story is important. This will indicate what age we should meet the character at and perhaps what age the character will be the majority of time we spend with them. Some stories take place in a short amount of time, over the span of a single day or even a single hour. Other stories span a character's life from the cradle to the grave. Still others cover a brief season of a character's journey. Unless you are writing an epic, you should likely only feature three seasons of a character's life – and usually fewer than that. In *Personal Shopper*, we meet a protagonist in one significant season of her journey. In *Lion*, we meet a character in two different seasons. And in *Moonlight*, we meet the protagonist at three very distinctive moments in his life. Many stories have featured men that we travel with from birth to the end of their days – but unfortunately few women have had that same treatment. In order to more fully understand the human experience, we sometimes need stories that capture the entirety of someone's life.

CONSIDERING STAGES OF LIFE

At various stages of human life, certain desires (and external goals) are more common than at other times. Babies, careers, and significance can be a part our lives of many different ages. However, there are certain times when these experiences are most common. There are other experiences that are universal and span across age groups – love, acceptance, and significance to name a few. Marking milestones in your story may be a helpful way to zero in on an age for your character as well. Births, weddings, divorces, and deaths all mark our lives in different ways. These milestones can work across genres as well. Bachelor and bachelorette parties have been one common marker in recent years. *The Hangover* films, as well as *Rough Night* and *Girl's Trip*, center their stories around the premise of a milestone at a specific stage of life. Different characters in a story will likely be experiencing different stages of their lives. However, the stage that the protagonist finds himself or herself in will interplay with the theme of the story, as well as the relationships they inhabit. Take care that all these moving parts function together well.

AGING YOUR CHARACTER EXERCISE

Create a timeline for your protagonist's life. Make the major events of their life on the timeline. Indicate where your story begins and ends on the timeline as well.

WEEK 23

LEARNING FROM POWERFUL ORPHANS

Certain archetypal characters seem to appear again and again throughout storytelling history. Many early narratives told tale of youngsters without one or both parents. From Moses to numerous fairy tales to Little Orphan Annie, orphans have served as heroines and heroes in countless stories, even when the plot does not specifically revolve around their abandonment. There's a moment in Wes Anderson's *Moonrise Kingdom*, when Suzie states that she wishes she were an orphan because most of her favorite fictional characters are. "Their lives are more special," she states. Psychologists have suggested that stories about orphans help us deal with the natural maturing process we all experience where we must come to terms with our own individuality and separate from our parents. Regardless of why, these characters have been some of the most beloved throughout history. Here's a list of beloved fictional orphans and what we can learn about creating our own characters, whether parented or not.

DAENERYS TARGARYEN – THE ORPHAN AS PARENT

A number of the characters in *Game of Thrones* are orphans including Jon Snow and Ayra Stark. However, it is Daenerys Targaryen that transcends her loss to become a powerful "parent" of her own as the mother of dragons. Professor X, in the *X-Men* series, an orphan as well, uses his pain to become a "parent" to others who have struggled with feeling like they don't belong, when he forms an academy for those with similar experiences. Wolverine, also an orphan, fills a comparable parental role in *Logan*.

JAMES BOND – THE ORPHAN AS SAVIOR

Many fictional orphans are handed a significant destiny as a savior of others. Orphan, James Bond builds a career doing just that. Harry Potter, an orphan, shares a similar destiny while Lord Voldemort channels his orphanhood in the opposite direction. Orphan, Frodo Baggins is called to be a savior in a realm beyond his humble life. Luke Skywalker, also an orphan, is called to save the entire galaxy. Rey and Finn, both orphans as well, pick up this mantle in later episodes of *Star Wars*.

CINDERELLA – THE ORPHAN AS OUTCAST

It's not surprising that many orphans are presented as outcasts in the narratives where they appear. While sometimes the banishment is from a systematic society, other times it is from those tasked with caring for them after the death of their parents. Cinderella is treated poorly by her stepmother and stepsisters. Snow White, also an orphan, suffers in a similar fashion. Orphan, Dorothy Gale feels outcast from the uncles and aunts caring for her, propelling her into her adventure looking for belonging in *The Wizard of Oz*. The ostracism is not always as dramatic as in the above examples. Clarice Starling, an orphan, has suffered as a subtler outcast – the rare woman in an organization almost exclusively comprised of men -- in *The Silence of the Lambs*.

JESSICA JONES – THE ORPHAN WITH A GIFT

A number of orphans in the story world have been given gifts beyond the natural abilities of human beings. While sometimes, this may be an exceptional talent, such as in the case of Will Hunting, many other times, the gift defies the natural laws of our universe. Superman has been gifted with abilities common to his home of Krypton, but uncommon on our planet. While Captain America and Spider-Man, both orphans as well, were technically born on earth, their giftings stretch beyond the natural world. Orphan Jessica Jones has a complex relationship with her own giftings and is called upon to investigate others with extraordinary giftings.

THE ORPHAN EXERCISE

Imagine that the protagonist in the story you are creating or would like to create is an orphan. How might this improve your story? How might it complicate your story? How might it change your story? Write two to three paragraphs exploring this possibility.

WEEK 24

IDEAS TO KICK START YOUR STORYTELLING THIS SUMMER

Summer is coming. Perhaps you've been thinking about beginning a new project and summer looks to be the perfect time to create it. Maybe you're thinking of breathing new life into an old story that's long been buried? You might be one of thousands of writers who began the new year with a resolution to finally get a story on the page this year, but haven't yet found time to get started. Knowing how to begin your writing practice, or begin it again, can be tough. Here are a few ways to begin to prepare *NOW* to kick start your storytelling this summer.

RESEARCH A NEW CHARACTER

Stories come out of characters. Far too many writers try to begin telling a story with characters whose lives they know very little about. Diving into a lifestyle, occupation, or era that you are unfamiliar with can be an invigorating experience. It can provide you with details about a person in that world that you wouldn't be able to describe otherwise. Researched characters feel more real. Charlie Hunnam portrays Percy Fawcett in *The Lost City of Z*. While the character is based on a real person found in a book by David Grann, Fawcett's character on-screen embodies details that speak to the research that James

Gray conducted to bring the character to screen. Gray was clearly familiar with the language, fashion, and customs of the period – things only discovered through good research. There are a number of ways to research characters outside of the obvious Google-related searches anyone can perform. Conducting interviews with individuals familiar with the world of your story is a good place to start. Another often-over-looked resource is the public library. Most of us assume anything found in a library can also be found on-line. While this is true of many things, it's not true of *everything*. Books, encyclopedias, newspapers, and a variety of other resources can be found in many libraries, but may have not piqued anyone's interest for scanning and being made available on-line. Many libraries also have free access to academic databases, journal articles, and back-dated periodicals that you have to pay to access on-line. Libraries also offer an environment for concentrating on research and writing. Getting away from the distractions found at home and in coffee shops can be a powerful way to welcome new narratives into your story world.

READ A HISTORICAL BOOK

Creators often only look to books as a source of inspiration for *adapting* a story. However, there are multitudes that can be learned by reading books that were either written *during* or *about* the period that you are setting your own story in. Sometimes beginning with a book from a historical period that you are interested in can be the catalyst in finding a great story to tell. While your reading may lead to an idea set within the time period of the era you are reading about, many times it will spark something best set in another time period. When constructing her iconic character, Frankenstein's Monster, Mary Shelley was vocal about having gotten the idea while reading a story set in a completely different period and world –*Paradise Lost*. Engaging in the way another storyteller has constructed a tale can sometimes be just what we need to unleash our own creativity, and often leads to unexpected results.

WATCH A FILM MADE BEFORE 1950

Many people go to the movies to escape. We, as storytellers, also occasionally need to escape to find ideas, characters, and stories that might not come to us otherwise. Taking ourselves out of the world of now and looking to a world we recognize but is a bit removed from us can help. Watching a film that you've never seen before, made before 1950, can function like a hard reboot for your storytelling. Looking for themes, archetypes, and storylines that would morph into relevance today can be like a narrative treasure hunt. Mining old classics for timeless truths is an enjoyable way to take spare time and make it resourceful. Alfred Hitchcock's 1929 film, *Blackmail*, originated many tropes common to crime thrillers in more recent times. Knowing what the storytellers who came before us have done successfully not only informs us of possibilities – it makes us better students of our craft.

THE KICKSTARTER EXERCISE

Choose one of the options above (or create your own kickstarter) and complete it within five days.

WEEK 25

STORY LESSONS FROM WOMEN SCRIPTWRITERS

In 2015, women made up only 9 percent of all directors on the top 250 films, according to San Diego State's Center for the Study of Women in Television and Film. That number dropped in 2016 to only 7 percent. Despite lots of discussion in Hollywood circles, the number of women directors remains abysmally low. Even less attention is given to the number of films and television shows *written* by women. Solid statistics on this topic are rarely tracked. It could be argued that this role is of even greater importance as the worldview and perspective of a story is found more profoundly in the script than in the directing. Here are five story lessons we can take from some of the top women writers in the industry.

NICOLE PERLMAN

-*HUMOR WORKS ACROSS GENRES*

Nicole Perlman penned the original *Guardians of the Galaxy* script, as well as *Sherlock Holmes 3*, and *Captain Marvel* films. *Guardians* jumped to mass success partly because it didn't take itself too seriously. Even in dangerous and violent landscapes, audiences enjoy seeing characters relieve the tension by making a few jokes. Regardless of the genre you are working in, there should be light moments that humanize the characters and remind us that they are people with multi-faceted personalities. Providing a little humor here and there can be a perfect way to do that.

AMANDA SILVER

-BUILD A WORLD FOR YOUR STORY

Amanda Silver launched her career in the horror genre with *The Hand that Rocks the Cradle*. She later moved into action adventure with *Rise of the Planet of the Apes*, *Dawn of the Planet of the Apes*, and *Jurassic World*. She recently completed the upcoming live-action *Mulan* project as well as *Avatar 3*. Silver has remained one of the top writers in the industry through her ability to construct a world on-screen. Though most of the franchises she has written for have been established in books or previous films, Silver has demonstrated an ability to bring the vision of a world to the screen through a unique lens. The worlds she has built make room for layered characters, loads of conflict, and line after line of interesting dialogue.

JANE GOLDMAN

-DON'T BE AFRAID TO GO BIG

Jane Goldman has proven to be a woman that knows how to write material that many assumed must be written by men – coming of age stories for male geek culture. She is responsible for *Kick Ass*, *X-Men: First Class*, *X-Men: Days of Future Past*, *Kingsman: The Secret Service*, *Miss Peregrine's Home for Peculiar Children*, and *Kingsman: The Golden Circle*. Goldman writes big stories, preferring large ensembles with intricate inner workings as opposed to small simple stories. While there certainly is a place for both, many writers are afraid to ever go big in the way that Goldman has. While her risks have been great, so have been her rewards.

GINA PRINCE-BLYTHEWOOD

-DEVELOP A STORY ECOSYSTEM

Gina Prince-Blythewood burst onto the scene with *South Central, Love and Basketball*, and later *The Secret Life of Bees*. She is also responsible for creating and writing the acclaimed television show, *Shots Fired*. While she has expanded the stories that she tells, Prince-Blythewood has continued to work in the same ecosystem of narratives that involve young African Americans (and often women) struggling to overcome the racially charged environments around them for a more meaningful and happier life. Continuing to work within this ecosystem has allowed her to deepen the stories she tells and perfect her craft to a level most still aspire to.

DIABLO CODY

-DON'T PLAY NICE

Diablo Cody won Best Original Screenplay for *Juno* in 2008. Since that time, she has continued to create fascinating characters and stories for both film and television. She is responsible for *The United States of Tara, One Mississippi, Young Adult*, and *Ricki and the Flash*. She is presently re-teaming with *Juno* director, Jason Reitman, for the upcoming *Tully*, as well as a film based on the *Barbie* franchise. Cody forged her way into the industry be refusing to create the stereotypical female characters that many audiences had become accustomed to, and instead creating fleshed out, real women, who sometimes refused to play nice. Great characters and stories reflect the reality of the human experience, which isn't always pretty. Sacrificing expectations for authenticity in screenwriting rarely goes unnoticed.

WOMEN WRITERS EXERCISE

Seek out the work of a woman that writes professionally. It can be someone listed above. Engage their storytelling and write two to three paragraphs about what you learned or observed in the way they told their story.

WEEK 26

SYMBOLS THAT CAN STRENGTHEN YOUR STORY

Good stories are like puzzles that the audience gets to put together both individually and collectively. Some pieces require a bit more searching when looking for where they fit into the whole. These pieces often offer the biggest emotional rewards for the audience. Taking a common object or image in a film and giving it subtext or additional layered meaning communicates to your audience on a level that pre-dates verbal language. There's a universality to the use of symbols. In short, they make your story stronger. Here are some commonly used symbols and a look at the way they get used in storytelling.

CLOCKS AND WATCHES

Clocks and watches are physical symbols of time. They can take on nuanced meaning about wasted time, lost time, remaining time, or even personal reflection, depending on the narrative elements surrounding the symbol. Stephen Strange sees his prized watch broken near the beginning of the story, symbolizing both the way his life has just changed in relation to his broken body, as well as the time he has wasted in the past in *Dr. Strange*. In *Pulp Fiction*, a wrist watch is also used but to much different effect. The watch delivered to young Butch by Captain Koons symbolizes the endearing love passed from one generation to the next but also the courage to withstand living nightmares – something the captain had to endure to get the watch to Butch. But also a symbol of the tenacity Butch will now need for the journey he is about to embark on. The film is ripe with other symbols, not the least of which is a brief case with mysterious golden contents. Clocks and watches are used throughout *Hugo* to take on a variety of different meanings while a watch is used in the dramatic conclusion of *Schindler's List* to symbolize the value of human lives.

GLASS

In the fields of mythology and depth psychology, glass often symbolizes that which is invisible – the divine, the soul, and those things that are clearly present but unable to be seen directly. In *Silence of the Lambs*, the glass that separates Clarice Starling and Hannibal Lechter symbolizes the invisible issues inside Clarice that separate her from the ugly truth. In a sense, two sides of herself are having a difficult conversation throughout the film with this safety glass to separate them. It is only after Lechter is no longer behind the glass and in the world she inhabits that she is able to solve her case and find freedom from her inner demons. Windows, in general, leverage the same sort of barrier between ourselves and the outside world. If we are standing outside already, they provide a portal that allows us a peek at the inside – all concepts rich in symbolic possibility. Mirrors are another type of glass, of course. They allow us to see ourselves as we truly are. They can also symbolize our most narcissistic side. Fairy tales often use mirrors as symbols as in *Snow White* and more broadly, glass in general, as with the slipper in *Cinderella*.

WATER

Perhaps the most ancient and common symbol, water represents cleansing, purification, movement, the unconscious, and a host of other interpretations. We see it used symbolically as rain, rivers, showers and baths, fountains, waterfalls, and even tears. In the opening image of *Election*, we see a water sprinkler dispersing its contents in a robotic monotonous fashion. It is a wonderful symbol of the life our characters are now experiencing – uneventful, the same every morning, directional, and seemingly without variety. In *Cast Away*, the ocean symbolizes both the greatest challenge as well as the greatest opportunity our protagonist has. It is his torture as well as his salvation. In *Indiana Jones and the Last Crusade*, our protagonist pours symbolic water on his father's wound, which heals him. It also represents the healing in the relationship between the two characters.

ANIMALS

If water is not the oldest symbol, that title would certainly go to animals. Throughout myths, fables, and folk tales, animals have represented every possible human emotion, condition, and basic characteristic. Nothing represents the human personality quite like an animal can. There is enough separation between ourselves and animals to remove the initial prejudices we hold. We can often see things portrayed between animals that we might not recognize among people. The cat that the protagonist chases throughout *Inside Llewyn Davis* symbolizes his dreams and fleeting career. The moment he is able to grasp the cat, it quickly escapes and runs away. The geese above his pond are what initially send Tony Soprano to therapy in *The Sopranos*. The therapist helps him to recognize they symbolize the potential loss of his family and his control over his own life. There's a symbolic deer in *Stand By Me* and another in *The Leftovers*. And who could forget the symbol of the horse's head in *The Godfather*?

While these are but a few examples, symbols surround us every day. We look for them even when we don't realize it. Looking for them as we go about our jobs and lives actually serves as a way to exercise your storytelling muscles. Symbols provide depth to our journey. They give life meaning. Their power in our lives make them equally powerful in our stories.

SYMBOLISM EXERCISE

Create two to three symbols that you could use in the story you are creating now or one you plan to create. Write a paragraph describing each symbol and how you will use it.

WEEK 27

USING NARRATIVE SHARDS FOR STORIES IN NON-TRADITIONAL MEDIUMS

Imagine the perfect story. Many of us dream of a story that features a motivated protagonist with a strong external goal, an equally compelling antagonist with a convincing moral argument, and dialogue rich with subtext and nuance. Envision all those ideal qualities contained within a single, beautiful, glass vase. Now, imagine dropping that story vase on the floor and watching it shatter into thousands of tiny shards. The narrative shards that cover the ground before you may just hold the secret to creating powerful stories, when your task is not easily defined. Many creators get asked to work on projects that fall outside the clean lines of the mediums they have previously worked in and knowing how to take the narrative shards of a good story and use them to craft a mosaic in any medium can be a life saver when we are called on to create characters, punch up dialogue, or create story elements for video games, interactive media, supplementary content, or any other place where storytellers may be asked to step in and lend assistance. Here are a few ways to use narrative shards.

CHARACTER SHARDS

At the end of the day, story is all about characters. Any concept will work for a few moments but without the help of a compelling character, even the best concept is all but dead. Leaning in to archetypal characters gives the audience a shortcut for understanding who a character is in a given scenario without much work on the part of the writer to set the character up. Wise old sages are archetypes used on stories from *Star Wars* to *Moana*. Faithful friends show up in stories from *Lord of the Rings* to *The Hangover*. Archetypes work for characters in every medium.

IRONIC SHARDS

Most every story benefits from creating a multiple series of set ups and payoffs. Those payoffs are even stronger when they are supported with some irony. The old adage of giving the audience what they are familiar with, just a little differently, holds true whether working on stories inside or outside of traditional mediums. Offering audiences a clue that a twist may be coming can lure the problem-solving areas of the brain into further engagement with the story. *Primal Fear* uses irony at the end of the story while *Venom* uses it at the beginning of the second act. Irony can be effective anywhere it's placed.

SYMBOLIC SHARDS

Audiences love meaning just below the surface of any story or narrative-driven scenario. Using seemingly insignificant objects and endowing them with meaning can touch the heart of an audience like few things do. Most writers are familiar with the symbolism of the sled in *Citizen Kane* but are you familiar with the symbolic shard of the red coat in *Schindler's List*? It's a bold creative choice that's worth investigating.

INCITING SHARDS

Every story needs a moment that propels the characters into action towards goals. We typically see this moment as the one where the story really starts. Some call it the inciting incident, others the catalyst, but this moment where the normal world of the narrative is suddenly changed is effective even when the story you are working on doesn't have three acts or any other expected tropes. Teddy accidentally burns down the retail store that he was about to become owner of in *Night School*, making the rest of his narrative journey possible. Having a moment that turns the world of the characters (or the audience) upside down can be an effective way of keeping the attention of viewers focused on where things go and how they will resolve.

MOTIVATIONAL SHARDS

Understanding *why* we should care about what a writer is telling us to care about is not only helpful, but often necessary. Watching Jennifer Garner maneuver in *Peppermint* is a good time without any context, but knowing she is doling out revenge on those that killed her husband and child makes the experience twice as sweet. Even without a stirring backstory, a simple understanding of motivation can help transform a ho hum narrative scenario into a complete thrill ride.

NARRATIVE SHARDS EXERCISE

Take a story you are currently working on or one you would like to tell and write two to three paragraphs about how you would bring that story into another medium. What narrative shards would you bring with you from your current story?

WEEK 28

TEMPLATES FOR CHARACTER ARCS

Seeing a character grow in her internal journey is one of the most effective ways to show that the character has arced. While a protagonist *learning* or *realizing* something is not effective as a visual external goal, these are powerful internal goals that, by necessity, characters are greatly unaware of while they are being subconsciously pursued. These processes of internal change are usually what we are referring to when we discuss a character's arc. The character arc can be simply explained as a character moving from one internal place to another. We might say it like this: The protagonist goes from being _____ to being _____. Identifying the beginning and ending place of your protagonist's arc is helpful in executing it throughout the course of your story. Here are several templates or examples of arcs that your character might go on.

She is a protagonist that goes from seeing the world in black in white to seeing the world in shades of gray

Knowledge of personality types are helpful when developing characters. Some personalities lean into binary thinking, needing the world to be simple and lacking in nuance. Of course, a brutal truth of life is that most issues are complex and involve shades of gray. Helping a character to discover this affirms the audience in their own considerations around complicated matters. The protagonist, Elizabeth, must confront this reality in *Miss Sloan*.

She is a protagonist that goes from solely taking care of others to also taking care of herself

The recognition that you can't provide for others what you haven't made room for in your own heart is central to the journey of protagonists with this arc. This process can be tricky to execute as the character may often need to continue to keep caring for others, if they are her children for example, but also find a way to have her own needs met. Alice Kinney navigates these waters in *Home Again*.

He is a protagonist that goes from being afraid to being courageous

This journey involves giving the protagonist tools to overcome his fear. Often these tools involve experiences and examples in the form of other characters. Sam Friedman becomes courageous over time through the example set by Thurgood Marshall in the film *Marshall*.

He is a protagonist that goes from having a closed heart to being open to love

The process of allowing your protagonist to open up his heart takes time and the involvement of another character that will make the risk worthwhile. Much of the journey will involve affirming the protagonist's timidity before something forces him to make a decision that puts all his feelings on the line. Andy in *The 40 Year Old Virgin* overcomes his avoidance of intimacy only after meeting Trish, the woman who could change everything for him.

She is a protagonist that goes from doubt to belief

Doubt is universal. All of us have issues that we face doubts about. Sometimes those doubts concern the values that society and those around us hold. Other times, the doubts we face are about ourselves. Belief occurs through the events that convince us of the reliability of certain ideas and values. Ellie journeys from a comfortable place of scientific doubt to a vulnerable place of belief in *Contact*.

She is a protagonist that goes from being naïve to being wise

Coming of age stories rely on the universal experiences of life to teach maturity. Moving a protagonist from naivety to wisdom takes time in the narrative. It involves the character making mistakes but then learning from them. Violet wises up after she moves to the big city and is taken advantage of in *Coyote Ugly*.

He is a protagonist that goes from being selfish to generous

While protagonists on this journey are often well off, this is not always the case. Sometimes, selfishness not only involves financial resources, but also time, or even affection as is the case with Vincent in *St. Vincent*. His journey is subtle and slow but ends with his character in a much different place than where he began.

CHARACTER ARC EXERCISE

Identify the beginning and ending place of your protagonist's internal arc. Use this template:

My protagonist goes from being _____ to being _____Write two to three paragraphs that unpack this journey.

WEEK 29

CAUTIONS ABOUT KILLING YOUR PROTAGONIST

Storytelling has always included tales where the protagonist dies before the story concludes. This can be a risky move for a creator to execute. It can make for a powerful moment of catharsis in the audience but it can also leave them confused or unsatisfied. Traditional story wisdom has told us that killing off your main character can be upsetting to the audience, causing them not to like the story. However, as new storytelling mediums have arisen, such as video games and virtual reality experiences, where a viewer *is* the protagonist on a journey who may be killed off, having the central character die has become more common. If you feel that killing your protagonist is the right narrative move in the story you are telling, here are a few cautions to consider in order to make sure you don't lose the people with the greatest investment in the story - your audience.

BUILD A SUPPORT TEAM

Ensemble stories have used this practice for a long time when a central character is killed off. In *Flatliners*, Elliot Page's character is presented as the central protagonist who initiates decisions that his cohorts are led by. However, time is spent developing each supporting character as well. When

Page's character dies near the end of the second act, there has been enough narrative constructed around the support team to complete the mission that he began. The closing image insinuates that he is with them in spirit, though not in body. The audience only feels a sense of resolution because the supporting characters have completed their journeys and arcs as well. *Saving Private Ryan* and *The Royal Tannenbaums* both build the journeys of their supporting characters in such a way that when the protagonist dies, the audience isn't left unfulfilled.

WAIT UNTIL THE END

Stories based around the journey of a single character are usually narratively over if that character dies. This can become stifling if your story is based on actual events and there are narrative beats that remain significant after the death of the protagonist. Moving the character's death as close to the story's conclusion as possible is often a wise move, leaving only the absolute necessities of resolution or reaction to the protagonist's death to play out. *Rogue One, American Beauty,* and *Braveheart* all execute this well. In Tom Cruise's most recent film, *American Made*, the protagonist is killed a few moments before the credits roll, reflecting the actual events that occurred. The filmmakers are then quick to give us a few lines of text that explain what happened to each of the supporting characters. A video recording that the protagonist had been making throughout the film allows him to have the final words in resolving his own story.

USE IT TO TRANSFORM OTHER CHARACTERS

The death of a protagonist can be powerful because of the impact it has on others. Demonstrating a legacy through a supporting character can be tricky, but will resonate with the audience if we too feel as though we've been transformed along the way. In *Titanic*, Jack's death has lasting impact on Rose, and thus on us, as the audience. In *Pay It Forward*, Trevor's death has impact on his mother and his teacher initially, but ends up impacting the entire community. In *Leaving Las Vegas*, Ben's death has transformational impact on Sera, his romantic partner, in somewhat the way that Jack's death functioned in *Titanic*. However, this is only one way to use the death of a protagonist to have impact on another character. In *Million Dollar Baby*, Maggie's death has tremendous impact on Frankie, even though she died by his hands and they were never romantic partners.

AN EXERCISE IN DEATH

Write two to three paragraphs about how it would impact the story you are creating (or one you would like to create) if the protagonist were to die in the story.

WEEK 30

DRAGONS EVERY STORYTELLER FACES

Dragons have captured our attention from the moment they stepped into our collective imaginations. These mythological representations of reptiles have appeared in virtually every culture's storytelling, dating back literally thousands of years. The Chinese dragon and the European Dragon have the most nuanced and discussed legacies, though the actual word *dragon* didn't enter the English lexicon until the early 13th century. Psychologists and other academics have suggested that the dragon represents a universal conflict that human beings all face. But do such deep examinations still apply in Disney films like *Pete's Dragon*? In a word – absolutely.

According to Mythologist, Joseph Campbell, the dragons of early lore were after two things – gold and virgins. The irony being, of course, that neither are of any use to dragons. They can't spend the gold and are unable to consummate their relationship with the princesses they capture. Still they hoard both in their caves until brave warriors or knights come to lay claim to them. Dragons are often used to represent the ego, which makes the desire for money and sex more understandable in the context of myths. *Pete's Dragon* represents a more complex view of dealing with the dragons in our lives – it suggests we respect and befriend them, but not be afraid of them or allow them to lord over us. Here are four character archetypes we've watched deal with dragons and what we can learn from each.

BEFRIENDING THE DRAGON

Pete in *Pete's Dragon*

It's easy to write this Disney film off as fare for children. However, to do so would be to miss an important self-examination, for stories about dragons are never *just* for children. Elliott, the dragon in the film, is clearly capable of destruction. This is an important element in the overall psychological journey of the narrative. If we are ever to befriend the dragon, we must first acknowledge it and what it's capable of. Acknowledging the part of ourselves that can be beautiful but also destructive if left unmanaged or threatened, is a necessary component of maturity. Every storyteller, and likely every person, has some element of who they are that has not arrived at full maturation. The quicker we can discover this part of ourselves and over time befriend it – the better chance we have of one day perhaps riding it through the clouds.

MOTHERING THE DRAGON

Daenerys Targaryen in *Game of Thrones*

Many of us come to recognize that the dragons that exist in our lives are actually products of our own creation. We have birthed them. We have fed and nurtured them. Yet, for some reason we are surprised when they begin to flap their wings, fly away from us, and breathe fire. Mother's must discipline their children. They must sometimes show tough love. Caring for the dragons that live inside of us can help us to maintain their loyalty as they themselves grow and develop. The dragon and the mother of the dragon begin to develop a relationship based on protection, mutual concerns, and love. Taking care of the dragons we birth in a healthy manner, can eventually produce healthy adult dragons that might one day care for and defend us in our own time of need.

SLAYING THE DRAGON

Bard in *The Hobbit*

While some dragons can be tamed and others can be befriended, there are dragons that simply must be battled and destroyed. It's a topic of much discussion among fans that Bard, and not one of the most central characters, is responsible for killing Smaug in *The Hobbit* series. There's an interesting lesson in Tolkien's storytelling, however. Those things in our lives that we weaponize in order to destroy the dragon within us may not be what can actually perform this task. Sometimes, the lesser known aspects of our identities are called in to serve major roles. Sometimes, there are those in our lives who hold the greatest solutions, who we may have never suspected. In many ways, Smaug is only slain through the efforts of a great many characters in the story. The person who pulls the trigger, or in this case releases the arrow, often gets the glory. However, their act, which should always be acknowledged can simply be the straw that broke the camel's back -- or slit the dragon's neck.

BECOMING THE DRAGON

Haku in *Spirited Away*

Miyazaki Hayao's classic story is full of mythological motifs and psychological underpinnings. One of the most interesting is when Haku is revealed as a dragon. As we often view our battles with dragons as external processes or internal journeys, we should remember that we are actually capable of becoming the dragon. Anakin Skywalker in the *Star Wars* saga individuates into his own dragon, of sorts, as Darth Vader. This is not uncommon for heroes. Seeing yourself in a mirror is the first step towards recognizing who you are and what you might have become. Self-analysis is a critical part of every writer's journey. Why am I telling the story I am telling? Why am I uniquely qualified to tell this story? Has my own ego turned me into a dragon, hell bent on delivering a story of my own makings as opposed to a narrative I am called to? When we make peace with slaying the dragon that has become us, we become capable of resurrection, transformation, and new heroic journeys.

DRAGON EXERCISE

Brainstorm about dragons, both literally and metaphorically. Write two to three paragraphs about the ideas you have and whether any realizations, especially the psychological ones, could influence the story you are working on now or one you would like to create.

WEEK 31

DISASTERS YOUR INNER ARTIST SHOULD EMBRACE

In 2003, Tommy Wiseau crafted what some called the worst movie ever made – *The Room*. The film quickly became a cult classic, running in midnight showings around the country. While initial reactions to the film broke Wiseau's heart, over time he learned to embrace his cult status, as well as the film's fame, even if it was for reasons that he objected to. Fourteen years later, The Disaster Artist tells the story of *The Room* and propels Wiseau's star into arenas never thought possible. It turns out the story of how *The Room* got made is actually more compelling than the film itself. There are some key lessons that storytellers can take from the situation. Here are disasters that your own inner artist should embrace.

Don't be afraid to let your story become something else

The narrative that Wiseau constructed around his own life and his film didn't pan out the way he hoped. It didn't take the shape he thought it should. And for some time, he could only push against audience reactions to his story. However, as he learned to open himself up to the fame the film gained, a new narrative rose. Sometimes, we have a character or a story that we are certain should be in a specific genre or medium of storytelling. When we open ourselves up to other possibilities, stories sometimes organically find their own way. David Lynch's *Mullholland Drive* was originally developed for television. When Lynch recrafted it into a feature film, another cult hit was born. Sometimes, the narrative kernel we have works, but we must open the grip we have around the specifics of the story to see it blossom into something more beautiful.

Go with your gut, even when everyone tells you different

One of the most difficult skills a storyteller can develop is the ability to discern when to listen to the wisdom of others and when to stick to their guns. Wiseau stayed with his own vision, which for many years seemed like a terrible idea. However, in the grand scope of things, now looks brilliant. If fame was Wiseau's ultimate goal, he has accomplished that, even if it was through a circuitous path. One of the most challenging aspects of listening to the opinions of others is that we often don't know what will turn out to distract us from where we were headed and what will re-align us with where we were going. Asking for input from others is a necessary part the creative process. It can be invaluable. However, artists and storytellers should also have the confidence to lean into their own instincts, even when they fly in the face of common opinion. Charlie Kauffman's *Eternal Sunshine of the Spotless Mind* is another story that might have never been told had he listened to the opinions of others.

Knowing structure is important. Breaking it can be a stroke of genius

Anyone that has read my work for any length of time knows that I am a proponent of story structure. I'm also a huge proponent of knowing when and how to break structure. Tommy Wiseau's path was unconventional to say the least. He didn't follow the rules that others said he needed to. In the end, it just might have paid off. Many storytellers ignore or break the rules of structure out of rebellion or ignorance. This is rarely effective. However, when a storyteller fully understands how story and structure works, and then decides to transcend that, the results can be magical.

THE DISASTER EXERCISE

Reflect for two to three paragraphs on some aspect of the story you are creating or an aspect of your creative process you might need to let go of. Writing about this doesn't mean you have to let go of it yet. It just opens up space to explore the possibility.

WEEK 32

HOW TO CREATE POWER DYNAMICS
IN YOUR STORY

The way that a protagonist moves through the world should be filled with challenges and tests of the ego. There is perhaps no better way to accomplish this than to thoughtfully create differences in power between your character and the others she interacts with. Because there are so many types of power in the world, the possibilities for how to execute the differences in power are nearly endless. When a character has less power than another, there are certain scenarios and emotions that rise. When a character has more power than another, an entirely different set of scenarios and emotions rise. Finally, when a character is on equal footing with another, the dynamic is also different. For example, comradery may exist between those characters, which is often executed through the use of a best friend or sidekick of the protagonist. However, it is also possible for a competitive dynamic to exist, as might be the case with two co-workers vying for the same job. When the power dynamics in a story feel natural and true to life, audiences will engage. When the power dynamics feel manufactured and artificial, they will not. Here are ways to create universal and archetypal dynamics in the story you are crafting.

Create Dynamics of Wealth, Class, Race, or Age

Power dynamics come down to difference. The more profound the difference between characters, the greater the opportunity for conflict, which is the path to emotional movement in the audience. Power dynamics based around things characters cannot change, such as race and age, can build to desires for fairness and justice in the mind of the viewer. Dynamics based on issues that can change throughout one's lifetimes, such as wealth and class, produce different feelings. Anger toward characters that exploit any of these factors in a story is a common reaction for audiences, which is a sign of investment in the narrative. In *Crazy Rich Asians*, Rachel Chu is confronted with several power dynamics when she meets her boyfriend's mother, who becomes her antagonist. Rachel is far less wealthy and from a completely different class, which her antagonist exploits for her gain. There is also an age gap between the two characters that creates a power dynamic, pitting spunky youth against traditional experience.

Create Dynamics of Experience

When one character has had a major success or made a major mistake, a power dynamic is created between her/him and the other characters. If the protagonist's experience was a success -- admiration, jealousy, and envy may surround the character. If the experience was a mistake -- shame and embarrassment may accompany their journey. When the protagonist is living under the burden of a heavy blunder, it creates struggles of self-worth, especially when characters affected by the mistake enter the story. In *The Happytime Murders*, The puppet protagonist has made a grand error before the story began. The dynamic between him and the other characters clearly exists as a result of that mistake, but we only learn the details and more clearly understand the relationships as the plot develops. As is common in stories with this dynamic, the underlying motivation for the protagonist is to restore the balance in power through some act of redemption.

Create Dynamics of Occupation or Position

Within any organization or company, there is a natural hierarchy of power. It is no wonder that stories are often crafted in these worlds. The dynamics automatically lend themselves to conflict and opportunities for exploitation. While there are a number of ways to explore a character confined to the dynamics that exist within the institution, they are a part of, one of the more common is for the protagonist to discover an injustice or oversight within their organization, that their position prevents them from correcting. Many times, in these stories, when the protagonist brings the issue to the attention of those that can affect it, the character is ignored, placated, or sometimes punished. This often "forces" the character the take matters into their own hands, upsetting the power dynamics of their occupation or position. This trope is seen across genres in a wide variety of stories from *Mrs. Doubtfire*, who must challenge the dynamics of the protagonist's position within his own home to *Mile 22*, where an elite intelligence officer must work outside the boundaries of his position and government organization in order to smuggle a mysterious man with sensitive information out of the country. While the character may suffer the consequences of the power dynamics at play, the reward at the story's end tends to be worth their sacrifice.

POWER DYNAMICS EXERCISE

Write two to three paragraphs exploring the power dynamics between the main characters in the story you are creating or one you would like to create. What gives one character power over another? Are the characters aware of these power dynamics? How do they feel about them?

WEEK 33

WOUNDS TO GIVE YOUR CHARACTER

One of the most fascinating and under-discussed characters in *Wonder Woman* is the villain, Dr. Poison. She is an intelligent woman, immersed in her work, but driven by hatred that causes her to develop vicious methods of inflicting pain on humanity. Her most striking physical characteristic is a mask she wears to hide the intense scarring she has suffered. The mask acts as a character trait and a metaphor for her inner psychic struggle. The mask exists to hide her *wound*. Many of the most intriguing characters carry a wound that they are either unaware of or struggle to keep from being seen. This is a universally used trope that not only draws audiences into the story but also causes them to consider their own inner wounding, which can be quite powerful. So, how do you organically incorporate a wound into a character's journey? What types of wounds connect most effortlessly with audiences? Here are a few wounds to consider integrating into who your protagonist is.

THE LOSS OF A PARENT

Nearly every member of DC's *Justice League* has a backstory that includes the loss of a parent. Batman, famously, saw his parents die at the hands of a thief outside of a theater. Superman's parents put him in a vessel launched into space before their own death on their home planet of Krypton.

Dorothy is being raised by her Aunt and Uncle, suggesting the loss of her parents in *The Wizard of Oz*. Disney often includes the loss of a parents in their character's backstories. *The Lion King*, *The Little Mermaid*, *Cinderella*, *Snow White,* and *Bambi* are just a few examples. Those interested in further examining this phenomenon would do well to examine the work of Joseph Campbell, who discussed the relationship between orphans and heroes.

THE BROKEN HEART

Storytelling history is filled with protagonists that suffer from love that went sour or has been lost. Often, this has led the character to avoid situations of vulnerability and new relationships. Almost without fail, the character's inner journey will involve the risks of learning to trust again. The catalyst in *Forgetting Sarah Marshall* is the heartbreak of the protagonist Peter Bretter. Rob Gordon in *High Fidelity* makes this same journey of learning to trust again. *Gladiator*, *As Good As It Gets*, and *Good Will Hunting* all feature main characters with broken hearts.

THE ULTIMATE MISTAKE

Regret is a universal human emotion. We all have moments and decisions in our life that we wish we could take back. This can also be a powerful wound to saddle a character with. One of Tommy Lee Jones's early film, *The River Rat*, tells the story of a character trying to put his life back together after being released from prison, where he served time for the biggest mistake he ever made. *Les Misrables* is perhaps the most celebrated story of a protagonist who spends his entire life trying to make recompense for an early mistake. *American History X* and *Unfaithful* both explore characters that spend the entire narrative trying to make amends for a mistake they have made which caused them deep wounding.

THE BIG SECRET

Secrets have the ability to fester and infect the human soul. Over time, secrets become wounds. When we are unable to live our full truths, we struggle to know true happiness and every accomplishment we achieve fills incomplete. Characters also suffer when forced to hide a secret. That secret might be love for someone else, an injustice we have committed, or even a powerful gift we have. The first two seasons of *The Office* often revolved around Jim's secret feelings for Pam, which he eventually reveals. Hannah Schmitz in *The Reader* holds a secret about her past that eventually wrecks her life as well as that of the young man at the center of the story. *Catch Me if You Can*, *Breaking Bad*, and *Dexter* all focus on characters with a big secret that encompasses their wound.

THE FAILURE

Failure is a part of life. How we respond to failure greatly defines our character and the way we see ourselves. Some failures develop into wounds we carry with us throughout our lives. Our characters can also carry wounds in the present that originate with a failure of the past. Roy Hobbs in *The Natural* suffers from a secret failure that sidelined him for more than a decade. *Back to the Future* deals with righting the wrongs of failures in our past. *Major League*, *School of Rock*, and *Little Miss Sunshine* all explore the failures in character's pasts and how we deal with tending to those wounds.

THE WOUND EXERCISE

Brainstorm about what wounds might suit the protagonist in the story you are creating or would like to create. Who are what caused the wound? How in touch is the character with the wound?

WEEK 34

ARCHETYPES TO BUILD STORIES FROM

Many storytellers confuse archetypes with stereotypes. While stereotypes confine who a character is, archetypes open up characters and cause us to relate to them on a deeply psychological level. They reinforce the mythic connection between an audience and the characters in a story. We see ourselves in archetypes. Author, Jonah Sachs said that when we encounter stories based on mythic patterns, it feels more like we are remembering something we've forgotten, as opposed to hearing something we never knew. Carl Jung suggested there were possibly as many archetypes as there were people in the world. While the definition of what makes a character archetypal may vary, most agree that they have a certain combination of traits we recognize and identify with on some level, even if we can't put our finger on exactly where we've seen them played out before. Here are several archetypes that can act as skeletons for designing a character. What sort of flesh, clothing, and rings you put on their fingers are up to you.

THE TENACIOUS WOMAN

With both implicit and explicit challenges railing against her, the Tenacious Woman soldiers on, overcoming chauvinism, doubt, and her own insecurities. Women portraying this archetype often are silent about their struggles until an event forces a reaction or the character decides she has had enough and decides to externally challenge her circumstances. Billy Jean King in *Battle of the Sexes* and Molly Carter in *Insecure* are examples of archetypally Tenacious Women.

THE MAN WITH A CODE

Right or wrong, the Man with a Code sticks to his guns. He does not allow the opinions or pressure of others to sway his methods or the justice he feels is due. Mike Ehrmantraut in *Better Call Saul* and Anton Chigurh in *No Country For Old Men* are both Men with a Code.

THE REGRETFUL OLD MAN

Haunted by the event(s) that caused him to make poor decisions, the Regretful Old Man is a mirror of wisdom for other characters, as well as the audience. *The Green Mile* and *Saving Private Ryan* both center around Regretful Old Men.

THE WISE OLD WOMAN

While a legendary archetype in Japanese culture, the Wise Old Woman is often sadly absent from Western stories. While she may not always get the starring role, she is sometimes found saving the protagonist from costly mistakes in cinematic narratives. Gil is given the secret to overcoming his inner demons when his Grandmother shares an anecdote about why she prefers the rollercoaster to the merry-go-round in *Parenthood*—a classic example of the Wise Old Woman.

THE TRIUMPHANT FOOL

Story guru, Blake Snyder, in his book *Save the Cat*, named an entire genre of films after this humorous and often inspiring archetype – the fool triumphant. Though unaware of it, the triumphant fool is a catalyst for change in the characters that she or he comes in contact with. *Forrest Gump* and *Being There* are both stories where the "fool" triumphs in the end, much to the delight of the audience.

THE UNDERESTIMATED EXCEPTIONAL

Overlooked by those around them, these archetypal characters often have an Achilles Heel that tends to get all the attention, until someone notices the brilliance hidden dormant inside of them. *The Soloist* and *Good Will Hunting* are both stories centered around the Underestimated Exceptional.

THE ARROGANT YOUNGSTER

This archetype is familiar to anyone who ever thought they knew everything, but eventually learned how little they actually knew. Many times, stories that revolve around Arrogant Youngsters are about their maturing over the course of the narrative, but not always. *Kingsman: Golden Circle* and *American Assassin* both offer Arrogant Youngsters who must face their own limitations.

THE BITTER LONER

Burned by society, those they love, or both, Bitter Loners tend to exist as warnings to the audience of the consequences of deep pain, poor decisions, or unhealthy choices. *Finding Forrester*, *Grand Torino*, and *Up* all feature Bitter Loners forced to confront what their bitterness has actually achieved them.

THE ARCHETYPE EXERCISE

Identify character archetypes that you find in the story you are creating or would like to create. Where have you seen these archetypes successfully executed before. Write two to three paragraphs about what you discover.

WEEK 35

FOUR (AMERICAN) GODS THAT CHARACTERS WORSHIP

The Starz Network's show, *American Gods*, has explored the idea that the gods of ancient times still exist, but have been weakened as people's beliefs became fixated on new gods – the cultural concepts that we have now come to worship. Author, David Foster Wallace once said that we all worship something. Communicating what your character worships, either explicitly or implicitly, gives us insight into her or his values, passions, desires, and even weaknesses. The themes of our stories often attempt to reconcile the worthiness of what the character worships. We all know that certain things should not be worshiped without consequence, because of the experiential truths we have lived in our own lives. When characters worship those things our culture has determined as unworthy, we expect an appropriate lesson to occur. Below are ideas that your character might worship as well as the likely outcome of their devotion.

MONEY

Almost every ancient religious tradition had something to say about the worship of money – mostly in the form of cautions and warnings. We all know that money can't buy happiness but we also all struggle with often feeling like maybe it actually can. At the very least, we know that money can buy things that make us happy, either in the short term or even long term. The complex nature of our relationship with money always makes this a topic worthy of our storytelling. In watching characters struggle with their own relationships with finances, we process our own. Showtime's *Billions* take a modern lens on wealth, influence, and corruption. *Wall Street*, *The Wolf of Wall Street*, and *Casino* have presented greed, and the worship of money, as being detrimental to happiness and security, while also being the reward for ambition and entrepreneurial success. The comedy classic, *Brewster's Millions*, reminds us that money can be both a blessing and a curse, as well as the central plot device for moving a character through an inner journey of self-discovery.

SELFISH PLEASURES

Much of life revolves around finding balance between the pleasures we enjoy and the obligations we must endure. Many of us work hard five days a week so that we might have two days to ourselves, seeking out own enjoyments. As with money, pleasures can be both positive and negative in our journeys, which makes them perfect tools for crafting struggles for our characters. There's certainly nothing wrong with pleasure itself. It's when pleasure becomes so selfish that it actually burdens or becomes harmful to others that it's destructive. Characters that pursue pleasure as the first and only priority in life are characters ripe for life lessons. In *About a Boy*, we meet a protagonist that has every pleasure a person could want, but when a child enters his world, he recognizes that nothing compares to the love that can be found in friends and family. Sometimes these pleasures can become addictions or even psychotic behaviors, as in *Leaving Las Vegas* and *American*

Psycho. Even in light hearted films such as *Arthur* and *Get Him to the Greek*, we find hedonists whose love of selfish pleasures hurt others, leading to comedic redemption.

TECHNOLOGY

The Age of Enlightenment and the Industrial Revolution drastically changed the way that people saw the world. Science and technology became gods elevated above many of the values that humans had held for millennia. Like so many other areas of life, when not placed in the proper balance, these powerful tools can drive us to forget about ideas that are equally, if not more, important. The archetype of the mad scientist embodies the caution characters should hold about worshipping science and technology. We see this with Doctor Finkelstein in *The Nightmare Before Christmas*, Dr. Howard Mierzwiak in *Eternal Sunshine of the Spotless Mind*, as well as in Will Rodman in *Rise of The Planet of the Apes*, Henry Wu *in Jurassic Park*, and most of the villains in the *Spiderman* franchise.

OURSELVES

Likely the most common of all the gods in the cinematic universe, as well as actual life, we tend to worship ourselves more than anything or anyone else. There are times in life when it is important to put ourselves first. As the FAA instructions before every flight emphasize, you should secure your own oxygen mask before trying to help others. However, when we put ourselves first exclusively, life becomes somewhat meaningless. Anyone who has achieved any sense of maturity has recognized that one of the greatest experiences we can have is putting someone else and their needs ahead of our own, sometimes even to the point of great sacrifice. In the classic *Casablanca*, Humphrey Bogart's character has been self-centered throughout the story, but is impacted by Ingrid Bergman, who he eventually ceases his own self-worship for, and offers a very tangible salvation. *The Hunger Games* and *Gran Torino* tell similar stories of characters that move from a form of self-worship to self-sacrifice. Jack Nicholson has played a number of characters whose arc involves dealing with self-worship, including his performances in *As Good as it Gets*, *About Schmidt*, and *Something's Gotta Give*. Bill Murray seems to appreciate this theme as well, with similar turns in *Groundhog Day*, *Scrooged*, and *St. Vincent*.

THE WORSHIP EXERCISE

Write two to three paragraphs about what your protagonist worships. Then write two to three paragraphs about what your antagonist worships.

WEEK 36

APPROACHES TO THE COMING-OF-AGE STORY

Coming of age stories have long been a staple of storytelling across mediums. Since the early days of film and television, audiences have enjoyed watching characters that mature before our very eyes. These stories usually offer hard lessons that only experience and living life can teach us. They usually focus on the growth of a character from youth into adulthood, emphasizing the internal development of that character as she or he navigates external situations. While the ways these stories are executed can greatly differ depending on the characters, the circumstances, and even the specific genre, there are some similarities between the most common approaches. Here are ways you might consider crafting a coming-of-age story.

THE MOMENT IN TIME APPROACH

The *Moment in Time Approach* explores the minutiae of characters' daily lives as a metaphor for their larger, and more profound, journeys. These stories often take place over the course of a single day or short period of time in the character's life. In Greta Gerwig's *Ladybird*, we meet a young woman whose daily struggle involves trying to fit in while also striving to leave her small-town life. In *The Breakfast Club*, we encounter a group of young characters that share a small seemingly insignificant experience over a single day together but learn an insightful lesson as a result. A group of young boys leave their neighborhood to go see a dead body in *Stand By Me*. They return well on the road to manhood as a result of the experience.

THE LONG-HAUL APPROACH

Much the opposite of the *Moment in Time Approach*, the *Long-Haul Approach* takes the prolonged view on the process of maturation. In these stories, we often encounter characters throughout various periods of their lives. We see them change as a result of the different seasons that they experience. In *Lion*, for example, we focus on two significant seasons of the protagonist's life – his early years of childhood and his mid 20s. Throughout the story, we are shown the connective narrative tissue between the two periods. *The Royal Tenenbaums* walks the audience through the humorous early years of its central characters in an extended montage. We are then brought into their adult lives and made to see how little they have changed. The story picks up at a significant moment of transition for all the characters in the story. The ultimate *Long-Haul* coming of age story is *Boyhood*, which follows a character, portrayed by the same actor, from early childhood through adulthood.

THE BIG EVENT APPROACH

Another method of developing coming of age stories involves the concentration around a single life event that forces growth and development in the story's characters. The key to successfully executing the *Big Event Approach* is to identify an event with enough gravitational force to affect every character in the story in some way. The event also must allow for an opportunity for growth and change. *American Pie* revolves around a collection of characters all trying to lose their virginity. Some fail in the quest and others succeed. However, all are changed as a result of the event. *Pretty in Pink* circles around a school dance and the relationships that lead up to it. When the dance does occur in the third act, we see just how much the characters have changed in the period leading up to it. *Juno* orbits around a pregnancy that affects the life, not just of the protagonist, but also everyone in her sphere of influence. The event serves as a catalyst for changes in the worldview of Juno and the characters she comes in contact with.

THE PETRI DISH APPROACH

The *Petri Dish Approach* is when a group of characters are put in close proximity, often a high school, and change as a result of their awkward fumbling when they "bump into each other." This approach requires conflict that results from the forced closeness that the characters' share. It has universal appeal as we have all been in situations where we had no choice but to deal with others in tight quarters, where escape was just not an option. *Clueless* explores the love, the drama, and the humor that arises when characters of highly competitive social classes are confronted with the lowbrow realities of high school. *Mean Girls* covers similar territory, but combines a "fish out of water" element. *Dope* explores the same idea but within the African American cultural experience. The *Petri Dish Approach* allows audiences to closely observe how we, ourselves, might grow in intimate circumstances where that growth does not seem evident at the time it's being experienced.

THE COMING-OF-AGE EXERCISE

Which of the approaches above resonates most deeply with you? Write two to three paragraphs about what you would explore if you were to tackle a coming-of-age story?

WEEK 37

PRINCIPLES FOR CREATING SOMEONE TO LEAD YOUR PROTAGONIST

Characters most effectively develop as a result of interacting with other characters. A standard trope in storytelling is that our protagonist will not figure out solutions to their conflicts on their own. They need experiences that will teach them what works and what doesn't. They need training that will prepare them for the ultimate battle that lies ahead. And they need other characters who can guide them towards victory. Sometimes these characters are mentors, teachers, or parents. Other times these characters are peers. Regardless of what social groups your character's guide comes from, there are a few principles that will help create an environment where the guiding character is both believable and effective.

THE SCARRED GUIDE

Giving the guide their own weaknesses, doubts, and failures makes the instruction and advice they give the protagonist more believable. We struggle to trust advice that has not come from someone who has been there. In *Queen of Katwe*, Phiona's chess coach, Robert Katende can help her navigate the ups and downs of her journey towards greatness because he comes from an even more difficult background than she does. Anything she faces, he has also faced, often in more extreme circumstances. His experience gives him credibility not only with Phiona but also with us as an audience. Amanda Waller of *Suicide Squad* and Nick Fury of *The Avengers* both serve as scarred guides for the heroes within their franchises. Even Mr. Miyagi in *The Karate Kid* is revealed to have a painful past of war and loss. His scars give him a deep well to draw from while guiding Daniel to victory both in the tournament and with his relationships. Doc Brown understands Marty in *Back to the Future* because he also knows what it's like to be shunned.

THE EXPERIENCED GUIDE

Every good teacher has also, at one time, been a good student. While we may accomplish the establishment of this in a variety of ways, demonstrating that the guide has lived through experiences that have taught him or her the lessons the protagonist needs to learn is important. Walt Kowalski in *Gran Torino* can speak into Thao's life because he has lived through similar experiences, though in a different culture. Patches O'Houlihan can advise a flailing dodgeball team, because he is an ex-dodgeball champion in *Dodgeball*. Irv Blitzer is basically the same character in *Cool Runnings*. John Keating has been a student just like the boys he leads in *Dead Poets Society*. Red's experience in *The Shawshank Redemption* allows him to guide Andy Dufresne which in turn allows Andy to guide Tommy. Perhaps the most memorable scene of any character touting their experience in the presence of an over-confident hero is in *Good Will Hunting*, when Sean Maguire, dramatically guides Will Hunting with his park bench speech.

THE MOTIVATED GUIDE

When the guide has their own reasons for wanting the hero to succeed, it brings a complexity both to their character as well as to the overall story. Sometimes the guide's motivation comes from an allegiance to a greater cause, as with Yoda and Obi-Wan Kenobi in the *Star Wars* saga. Sometimes, it originates from selfish motivations as with Jack Donaghy's mentoring of every aspect of Liz Lemon's life on *30 Rock*. Other times it comes from a place of compassion as with Giles, the mentor figure in *Buffy the Vampire Slayer*. Many times, the motivation for the guide comes from nepotism, as with Uncle Ben in *Spiderman* or neo-nepotism as with Alfred in *The Dark Knight*. Charles Xavier in *X-Men* is driven to guide his students by his own dream to see humans and mutants live together in peace. Frankie Dunn is a reluctant guide at first but transforms into a very motivated guide after seeing the tenacity of his student in *Million Dollar Baby*. Dumbledore of *Harry Potter* lore and Gandalf of *The Lord of the Rings*, both serve as guides from a place of position. They both feel a sense of duty because of *who* they are.

A FINAL CHALLENGE

I am often disheartened to find a great lack of female guides in storytelling. Even when the protagonist is female, it seems that the guiding character is often male. *The Devil Wears Prada* and *Miss Congeniality* both feature wonderful gay mentors for our protagonists, which is different than what we often see, but still, they are male. Some have pointed to the Pygmalion myth and its never-ending presence in storytelling as the reason behind a lack of female guides. So, I conclude with this challenge for *all* writers. Find opportunities to use female characters as guides for female *and male* characters. This is a gaping hole in the quilt of storytelling that we should begin repairing immediately. I look forward to seeing how you step up to the challenge.

THE GUIDING MENTOR EXERCISE

Consider a guiding mentor for the story you are creating or one you would like to create. If you have already created such a character, consider the repercussions of making that character a woman. Write two to three paragraphs about how this could impact your story.

WEEK 38

THE FAUSTIAN BARGAIN: DEALS YOUR CHARACTER MIGHT MAKE WITH THE DEVIL

In the classic story by Goethe, the character Faust makes a deal with the devil, exchanging his soul for knowledge. The idea of a Faustian Bargain, sometimes called a Faustian Pact, has long been a trope of storytelling, where the willingness to abandon one's principles or eternal value for worldly benefit speaks the unquenchable thirst for power. While selling one's soul to the devil has made a great literal plotline for thousands of stories in the past, the basic concept of an exchange or trade based on limitless desire also holds plentiful variations and metaphoric possibilities. Here are a few deals your character might make in order to get what they want in your story.

EXCHANGING THEIR OPPORTUNITY FOR PRIDE

Pride has kept almost everyone from something they truly desired in life. It's a universal experience. Our characters will likely make the same mistakes. Pride may keep us from the apologies that make a relationship possible, the humility that often accompanies hard work, or the risks that could embarrass us in a vulnerable moment. In order for a character to succeed, they will likely need an opportunity. In many stories, the character's pride will be what prevents them from taking advantage of that chance, setting up a lesson that may take the entire narrative to learn if they ever learn it at all. In *Chappaquiddick*, Ted Kennedy exchanges the potential to one day become president for the pride that would be lost in readily admitting a life-altering mistake.

EXCHANGING THEIR DIGNITY FOR SURVIVAL

Some exchanges are the result of impossible circumstances. They occur when a character feels like they have no other options. In the most extreme cases, a character may feel they even have to sacrifice the dignity of their body for their own survival or the survival of someone they love, as with Fantine's character in *Les Misérables*. In other stories, a character's dignity may be sacrificed for survival in a toxic workplace as with Andy's character in *The Devil Wear Prada*. Where traditional Faustian Bargains usually involve an exchange that takes advantage of a character's greed, this exchange only occurs as a result of the character's desperation.

EXCHANGING THEMSELVES FOR ANOTHER

In a similar selfless exchange, a character may sacrifice themselves for another. This might involve sacrificing one's opportunity so that another might have it. It might also involve the laying down of one's life for the good of others. In *The Iron Giant*, the kind-hearted mechanical character offers up his own existence in the final moments of the story to save those that he has come to care about. Exchanging one's self for another is the greatest act of love a character can demonstrate. It must be used sparingly and only in circumstances that have been properly set up throughout the course of the story, often beginning with moments where the character has acted selfishly.

EXCHANGING THEIR POWER FOR GREED

The desire to have more than we need is common across cultures and throughout history. This desire has been the downfall of many individuals, both real and fictional. Sometimes, our lust for more consumes us to the point where we are willing to give up our own agency and ability to control our own journey. Our ultimate power comes in our ability to make choices and have some degree of say in our own destiny. When an individual gives that up, feeding their own greed, redemption becomes extremely difficult. *The Wolf of Wall Street* and *There will be Blood* both highlight characters who eventually trade their own power and agency for the possibility of having more money than they could ever spend. In both cases, it leads to their destruction.

EXCHANGING ALL THEY HAVE FOR HOPE

With the character of Faust, trading his soul was symbolic for trading all he has and will ever have. While Faust's trade was driven out of his own narcissism, exchanges where a character offers up all they have can also be driven out of the noble motivation of hope. Coming to the bargaining table with everything one has and could ever have is risky. It creates stakes that will keep the audience on the edge of their seat. In the final moments of *Casablanca*, Rick exchanges all he has to protect a woman he once loved (and perhaps still does) and her husband from the Nazis. In his parting words to her, we find the hope that he has received in exchange – a hope that has replaced the cynicism that he carried throughout the story until she re-entered his life.

THE FAUSTIAN EXERCISE

What deal might the protagonist in the story you are creating (or thinking of creating) make to get what they want? What are the dangers involved in such a deal?

WEEK 39

HOW TO USE WEATHER IN YOUR STORY

Depending on where you call home, the weather may be cooling off right now. Most writers enjoy crafting their stories in nice comfortable rooms that are cool when it's hot and warm it's cold. Because we usually seek out a pleasant environment when we write, it's easy to forget the role that weather can play in our stories. Sometimes, the weather can even become a character itself in the narrative. Here are different ways that weather can be used to add conflict, build intensity, or affect fortunes in your story.

MAKE IT RAIN

Certainly one of the most dramatic visual experiences we encounter as humans is when water falls from the sky. While we now take for granted the science behind the phenomenon, for centuries rain was a great mystery that connected people to their gods and transcendent fate. Even with our complete understanding of rainfall today, most of us have gotten caught up either the wonder or the horror of a particularly rainy day. Akira Kurosawa used rain to great effect and meaning in both *The Seventh Samurai* and *Rashomon,* where rain symbolized the pure truth falling from the heavens that every character was trying to avoid. *Blade Runner, The Perfect Storm,* and *Jurassic Park* all use rain to intensify the experiences of the characters in those worlds. *Magnolia* literally rains frogs from the sky in an act of Biblical judgement and mysterious symbolism, and who could forget the iconic image of Andy Dufresne standing, hands raised to the sky, as redemption rains down on him outside the gates of Shawshank.

MAKE IT OVERCAST

Perhaps rain is not the right fit for your story. Perhaps it's too dramatic, ominous, or complicates other scenes in the script. Gray and overcast skies can also allude to the metaphoric conditions that characters can find themselves in. Patty Jenkins brilliantly uses gray skies in a variety of ways in *Wonder Woman.* While some scenes use overcast heavens to show the darkness of the times, other scenes use the skies as a promise of hope in a rising dawn. *A Series of Unfortunate Events, Sleepy Hollow,* and *Harry Potter and the Goblet of Fire* all feature overcast scenes that seem to predict a coming storm in the world of the protagonist. *Shame, Fight Club,* and *The Matrix* all use gray skies to indicate the condition of the environment the main character feels trapped inside. While *Eternal Sunshine of the Spotless Mind* and *Silver Linings Playbook* both use cloudy skies as a catalyst that calls the hero toward change.

MAKE IT HOT

When it's cold outside, we can always put more clothes on or cover up under blankets. When the heat is unrelenting, there's only so much clothing we can shed or cool water we can drink. Heat can bring a desperation to a story in ways that no other element can. Hitchcock famously used the heat to intensify the setting of *Rear Window.* The Cohen Brothers made a similar play in *Barton Fink*. Both *Dog Day Afternoon* and *Falling Down* use the heat to symbolize the inner thermometer of the protagonist as the story progresses. Spike Lee has used extreme temperatures in several of his films to different effects. *Summer of Sam* uses the weather to create a boiling kettle of accusations in a community. While *Do the Right Thing* uses the same extremes as both a symbol of everyday life in a neighborhood as well as an unsustainable condition that eventually must explode.

MAKE IT COLD

Like the rain and the heat, cold temperatures can be used as a wonderful symbol for the inner experience of a character or the metaphoric conditions that she or he finds themselves in. *Winter's Bone*, *Fargo*, and *Let the Right One In* all use cold weather to symbolize the obstacles the protagonist is facing in their inner journey as well as providing an obvious external level of discomfort and challenge. Both *Misery* and *The Hateful Eight* use cold weather as a prison that forces characters to collide with each other in unavoidable circumstances. *The Ice Storm* uses ice and cold weather to paint a picture of the fragility, awkwardness, and pain in young people working through the coming of age.

MAKE IT DISASTROUS

Some stories use extreme weather as the basis for the plot itself. While the disaster may or may not have larger symbolism attached to it, the pure external nature of seeing human beings collide with the most natural elements we have faced since the beginning of time remains ripe ground for storytelling gold. *Twister* uses tornados. *San Andreas* uses earthquakes. *The Impossible* uses tsunamis and *The Day After Tomorrow* uses virtually every natural disaster one can experience. It's important to remember, however, that sometimes weather disasters can actually be used in light hearted ways as well. *Cloudy With a Chance of Meatballs* connected with audiences of all ages and used the intriguing but ludicrous idea of food falling from the sky – a weather phenomenon that most of us would at least be curious to experience.

THE WEATHER EXERCISE

Choose three different scenes in the story you are creating or in a story you have created in the past. Write a short paragraph about the weather in each of these scenes. Even if the weather doesn't play into the tone or feel of the scene, describe it anyway.

WEEK 40

STORY LESSONS FROM MONSTERS

The announcement and subsequent loss of Universal's Dark Universe, where they planned to revive classic monster franchises, brought a wide range of reactions from around the storytelling world. For those unaware, the plan was that a new series of movies around the classic monster characters owned by the studio would be released in much the same fashion as Marvel and DC brought their cinematic universes to screen. Even though the plan has since been scrapped, the fact that certain monsters have had extremely long careers in the world of storytelling is undeniable. So, what is it about these characters that audiences can't get enough of? Are there elements found around the archetypes these characters rise from that give them their popularity? Here's a brief look at some of the most classic monsters in cinema and what we can draw from them that might be useful in our own stories.

THE MUMMY

Mummies have long been a staple of storytelling, especially in the film world. Mummies have faced our greatest fear – death – and somehow managed to come back. They cling to life in a way that we universally relate to. The cloth wrapping that surrounds their bodies hides how they truly are, yet the shape of their form can still be seen. The metaphors that mummies embody for us are many. Perhaps most significantly, mummies represent those things we fear but can't quite see in their true form – things that are covered and hidden. As Hitchcock stated, sometimes what we can't see is far scarier than what we can.

DRACULA

Desires and Cravings make characters realistic and relatable

Perhaps the best known of all monsters, Dracula has been presented as scary, relatable, and even sexy in the story world. Of course, Dracula got his start in the pages of a novel. While images and characteristics of Dracula have changed with the times, the singular quality that always remains is his craving for blood. All the dark count does is in pursuit of that he most wants. He is driven by his desire. Cravings are universal. Some things we crave because we need them, such as food, water, and shelter. Other things we simply want. And some of us want these things more than others. Good stories are often born out of characters that want something badly and are willing to go to great lengths to get it. The more ravenous we make our character for what they desire, the more invested the audience becomes in seeing that character get what they are searching for.

FRANKENSTEIN

We empathize with tension between the interior and exterior

Mary Shelly's monstrous creation has likely been psychologically analyzed more than any fictional creature. Though technically it is the doctor named Frankenstein and not the monster, the culture at large has come to refer to him by his creator's name.

Crafted together with spare parts, the monster is a collage of various elements from others, which is itself a wonderful metaphor for how some of the most beloved characters are created. The most relatable aspect of the monster, however, is that he is misunderstood. He is not the evil creature that everyone assumes on seeing him. His ghastly appearance causes people to run in fear from him before ever asking a second question. Only a young blind girl gives him a chance, unable to see his haunting exterior. Frankenstein's monster is a living example of the struggle between the interior life and the exterior life. Despite the many cultural warnings about judging a book by its cover, everyone has known the pain of seeing that warning ignored. Characters should be living with a certain amount of inescapable tension. This monster teaches us how to do that.

THE INVISIBLE MAN

Using the Power of Feeling Seen

You've probably been asked before if you could select between the ability to fly and invisibility, what you would choose. It's be suggested that your answer says something about your own wounds and inner psychology. While many fantasize about the voyeuristic opportunities that being invisible might offer, not being seen in cinematic stories has made one a monster. Loneliness and despair are often associated with The Invisible Man. Finding ways to express these feelings in characters, either metaphorically or explicitly opens up a universal connection with the audience. Many monsters are based on our own deepest fears of what may be true of ourselves. The Invisible Man is just such a monster. From him, we learn that it's not enough to simply see others, it is essential in life that we feel seen as well.

THE MONSTER EXERCISE

Write two to three paragraphs about your relationship with monsters. Do you have a favorite? Are you abhorred by the concept? Has your relationship with monsters changed over time? What do you think this relationship might say about your own psychology?

WEEK 41

THE DEVIL IN THE DETAILS: *How to Use Details to Add Layers to Your Story*

Imagining worlds is one of the most rewarding aspects of telling stories. We see people and places in the eye of our mind, complete with specific costumes, vivid landscapes, and precise hues. Many creators revel in including these details in their stories. And while a meaningful description of a character's physical appearance can create realism in the audience's mind, too often the details included in the descriptions of characters and the worlds they inhabit don't add any additional layers or meaning to the story and become a distraction that weighs the narrative down with unneeded verbiage. The details we include in a story can bring it to life and make it feel more authentic. But when details don't seem to tell us more about a character's psyche and inner life or the nuances of the environment they live in, audiences can get frustrated by too much minutiae. Here are ways to properly use details in your story to draw an audience in, rather than isolating them.

USING COLOR

One of the most tempting ways to describe an object or an environment is to begin with the color. Some writers simply mention that a character's shirt was green. Others will describe a peaceful pasture divinely painted in shades resembling the spectrum of the world's emeralds. There are times and places where each method may be most appropriate. Regardless, the use of color should tell the audience something that will matter in the story at some point. Drew Goddard's script for *The Martian* opens like this:

```
THE RED PLANET momentarily eclipses the Sun.
As sunlight breaks across the edge, warming
the surface...
```

Telling us the planet is red is not just a fun detail. It communicates that we are looking at Mars, the setting for our story, and begins to paint an image that establishes the palette for the environment of the film. Jim Uhls uses a similar technique when introducing the character of Marla Singer in *Fight Club*. She is described like this:

```
MARLA SINGER enters.  She has short matte black
hair and big, dark eyes like a character from
Japanese animation.
```

Telling us her hair is matte black, rather than a shiny black or just simply black communicates that her character has a worn sense to her – that she does not prefer the flashy. Uhls doesn't just repeat that her eyes look black as well, but gives us a simile to provide even more insight into who she is. Patti Bellantoni's book *If It's Purple, Someone's Gonna Die* is a helpful resource for those wanting to dig deeper into color theory and the meaning behind hues in storytelling.

USING DIALOGUE

The smallest comment or mention of something in dialogue can have huge impact if implemented correctly. While it is important to avoid being too on the nose with dialogue that reveals the inner world of a character, what a character says can tell us a great deal about who they are. In Taylor Sheridan's *Hell or High Water*, we can see an example:

```
              TANNER
              Put the gun on
              the counter??
              You liked to get
              us killed!

                        TOBY
              I'm not stealing
              from some old
              man. We stealing
              from one place.
              That's it.
```

But Tanner isn't angry, he's laughing.

```
              TANNER
              You're turning
              out to be a poor
              criminal.
```

When Toby tells Tanner that he won't steal from old people or multiple places, we understand that he is reluctant to steal at all – that he'd rather not be doing this and has a code for how far he will let this take him. These details in the dialogue tell us a great deal about what sort of man he is in a very short amount of time. This is powerful and efficient writing. In *The Fault in Our Stars*, Scott Neustadter and Michael H. Weber open up their protagonist, Hazel, in a similar way through dialogue:

```
              DOCTOR
              I may switch
```

```
                  you to Zoloft.
                  Or Lexapro. And
                  twice a day
                  instead of once.


                  HAZEL

                  Why stop there?


                  DOCTOR

                  Hmm?


                  HAZEL
                  Keep 'em coming.
                  I can take it.
                  I'm like the
                  Keith Richards
                  of cancer kids.
```

Hazel's joke tells us that she has become jaded about her illness but still has her sense of humor. It also tells us that she doesn't think those entrusted with her care really understand her. We are given insight into Hazel's inner life and worldview with just a few off-handed details in the dialogue.

USING SYMBOLISM

Symbolism can be a powerful way to communicate the theme in a film as well as understandings about what a character wants, desires, and loves. Often times, an object will hold great significance in the overall narrative. It becomes a totem of sorts. Charles Foster Kane's sled, Rosebud, in *Citizen Kane* is perhaps the most famous symbol of this kind ever used in film. These symbols are usually most effective when their meaning is revealed over time in the narrative, but not always. We are given the meaning of Butch's watch before we see the lengths he will go to get it in *Pulp Fiction*. We would do well to remember that while symbols might be most common in dramas, symbolism can work across genres. In Tim Herlihy's *The Wedding Singer*, the protagonist's Van Halen shirt becomes a symbol for his affections. When his new girlfriend sees his former fiancé wearing the shirt, she is led to believe he has fallen back in love with his ex. The detail of the shirt not only tells us what band he likes, but also acts as a symbol of his love.

THE DETAILS EXERCISE

Select a scene from a story you are working on now or one you have crafted in the past. Insert three details into the scene that expand the meaning of the scene or the depth of a character in the scene.

WEEK 42

CURES FOR THE 3ʳᴰ ACT BLUES

Audiences care about how they feel when they experience your story. They can love your opening scene, stay engaged through every beat of your character's struggle but if things don't feel right in the final moments of your story, even the most devoted story lover will be disappointed – and that pressure can be enough to keep a creator from committing to an ending. Here are three approaches for tackling the final section of your story.

GO BACK TO THE FUTURE

Most storytellers get stuck in the 3rd act of their story because of a problem with their 1ˢᵗ act. They end up trying to answer a question that was never really asked at the beginning of the story. One way to avoid this issue is to outline the entire story you are telling. Even the most seasoned storytellers run into problems where the execution of the story led to a different place than what was originally planned. Sometimes, even with all the right intentions we end up at the end of the 2ⁿᵈ act and are not sure exactly how things should go. Returning back to the first act almost invariably addresses the issue. You cannot pay off what you did not set up well. If we pay close attention to the 1ˢᵗ act in *La La Land*, the 3ʳᵈ act is clear from the beginning, but it never keeps us from enjoying the journey along the way. Similarly, we know how things will turn out in the 3rd act of *Patriot's Day*, if we are familiar with the historical event. However, it's the thematic questions asked about who the characters are in the 1st act that must be addressed to complete the story for the audience. In many ways, good stories are somewhat circular. We return to the gaps we begin with, fill them, and only then is our story complete.

DELIVER ON THE PROMISE

Visual stories often make grand promises in their trailers, posters, and on-line ads. If we see Tom Cruise running in the trailer, we expect to see him jump out of or into something exploding, when we go see the film. If we see Charlie Day on a poster, we expect he will get himself into and then promptly out of some serious trouble – we just want to know how. Most stories give us some indication of what we can expect to feel at the end of the story. Great dramas may promise challenge, heart ache, or inspiration. Comedies always promise laughs. Horror films promise jumps and scares. Action films promise adrenaline. Knowing what the genre of your story is acts as the first step in getting some idea of what your film should promise. However, this is only a place to start. Comedies promise laughs, but they promise laughs throughout the film, and the reassurance of a satisfying and sometimes sweet ending. Action films promise adrenaline, but also that the heroine will find a way out of the mess she is in during the 3rd act. *Sleepless* promises lots of car chases, shoot outs, and general bad assery from Jamie Foxx. But we also expect to see him overcome the villain and live to fight another day in the 3rd act. *Why Him?* promises laughs by the load from its two incompatible main characters, but we also expect to see them find a way to get a long for the sake of the woman they both love, in the 3rd act. *Jackie* promises insight into the complexity of the woman's life. Even with a story many viewers are familiar with it, the writer manages to convey the promised insights. Whatever your story has promised in the first two acts, or should have promised, the third act must now deliver on.

PLAN A SURPRISE

Suppose you don't want to deliver what your audience expects in the 3rd act. Suppose you want to hit them with something they don't see coming. First, know that audiences are very picky about the surprises they like. They can often get upset when a writer gives them the unexpected in the 3rd act. However, when executed well, a surprise in the 3rd act can have more emotional impact than any other ending. The key to a successful surprise in the 3rd act is to plant evidence along the way. Audiences love to feel like they had clues all along, but never picked them up. This can be tough to deliver on, however, as audiences have also become so savvy that burying clues has becomes a real challenge. When looking at your own story, ask yourself what the audience would never expect in the 3rd act? What would be the worst thing that could happen to your protagonist? Is there a character in your story who could turn out not to be who we believed he or she was all along? Edward Norton's 3rd act reveal in *Primal Fear* launched his career as did M. Night Shyamalan's in *The Sixth Sense*. Audiences didn't respond so kindly when Shyamalan used the same technique with *The Village*, however. The 3rd act surprise can be a tightrope. Proceed with caution.

THE THIRD ACT EXERCISE

Brainstorm three possible endings for a story you are working on or one you have told in the past. What is the expected ending? What would be an ironic ending? What would be a completely unexpected ending?

WEEK 43

HOW TO CRAFT A SURPRISE ENDING

Surprise endings can be tough for storytellers. First, they take a certain amount of cleverness and inspiration that cannot just be conjured up out of thin air. Next, they must work in that delicate space where the audience has been given some subtle clues about what will happen, yet not so many clues that the reveal has become obvious to most viewers. Here are tips on how to craft a surprise ending for your story.

THE SURPRISE PLACE APPROACH

With this approach, the audience comes to realize they are not *where* they think they are. Orientation is one of the most basic concepts an audience holds when watching a film. Finding out that the story has been taking place in an unexpected location can be thrilling. We've seen a wide variety of ways this approach can be executed to great effect. In *Being John Malkovich*, interesting locations keep the audience guessing as to their relationship with reality. While having a film take place inside someone's head can be risky, as establishing "rules" for this "world" are often difficult. When handled delicately, the payoff can work brilliantly. In *The Planet of the Apes*, the location reveal at the end of the story, causes us to reconsider everything we believed about the philosophy of the characters as well as their backstories. Of course, no discussion about surprise endings would be complete without mentioning M. Night Shyamalan. While some love and others loathe *The Village*, it certainly has a surprise locational ending that fooled many.

THE SURPRISE PERSON APPROACH

With this approach, at least one of the key characters are not who the audience believes he or she is. This is the most commonly used method for crafting a surprise ending and the examples of its power are many. In *Fight Club*, we find out the protagonist and antagonist are actually two sides of the same personality. In *Psycho*, we find out the antagonist has been dead for years and is actually another character in disguise. In *The Prestige*, we find out one of the main characters is actually two different people. *The Usual Suspects* and *Primal Fear* both feature characters that turn out to be much more evil than the sweethearts we have believed them to be. And who could forget the most shocking character reveal of all time – when the epitome of cinema badness, Darth Vader, turns out to be our hero's father.

THE SURPRISE ASSUMPTION APPROACH

While more rare than the other approaches, ending your story by challenging the assumptions your audience has taken for granted can be a powerful way to conclude the narrative. Like pulling the rug out from under the place or people the audience has come to engage with, the assumptions we make about characters and the structure of the story its self can provide a stale story with unexpected irony. In *The Book of Eli*, we are shocked to learn the man with the vision to lead has actually been blind the entire time. Viggo Mortensen's character in *A History of Violence* baffled the audience when the assumptions we have made about the nature of his character are quickly upended. More recently, audiences were taken with the surprise ending in *Arrival,* when they learned that scenes we assumed were flashbacks were actually flash forwards. Tinkering with the structural pillars of your story can be dangerous, especially when you might not have Amy Adams to execute the nuances of such risks. But occasionally these gambles can be just what a script needs to take it from good to great.

THE SURPRISE EXERCISE

Brainstorm three surprises that you could reveal in the story you are currently working on or on a story you would like to tell. Even though you might not use any of the surprises you come up with, this exercise may help you begin to think differently about the possibilities in your story.

WEEK 44

HOW TO USE IRONY IN YOUR STORY'S ENDING

While irony can be an effective tool throughout your story, there's perhaps no time it has greater impact than at the conclusion. Irony is not just about tricking the audience by revealing something they never saw coming. It is also an instrument that can be applied subtly to reinforce the reality of how life can thwart our plans, intentions, and dreams. Of course, not all irony results in unhappy endings. Sometimes, especially in romantic comedies, protagonists are faced with the ironic realization that the type of person they deeply need has been at their side all along in the form of a close friend. However its executed, irony is most effectual when it is somehow tied to the protagonist's wants or needs. Here are a few ways to use irony in the final scenes of your story to move your audience's expectations and emotions.

THE HIDDEN GIFT

The protagonist gets what they need but not what they wanted

With this ending, the protagonist learns a valuable lesson – sometimes what we want and what we really need are two different things. Though the heroine may ultimately fail at achieving her external goal, she manages to secure the thing that meets her deepest internal need, which turns out to be much more valuable. In *Bridesmaids*, Annie *wants* to be Lillian's best friend. However, now that Lillian is getting married, she is devoting more of herself to her husband and has made new friends that also feel strongly about Lillian. Annie humorously, and tragically, demonstrates she is willing to destroy any competitor in order to get what she wants from Lillian. This causes her to lose what she has wanted so desperately. The hidden and ironic gift given to Annie at the end of the story is that her most viable competitor offers her the deep friendship she wanted from Lillian. A theme emerges suggesting that what we most long for may be waiting in the most unlikely of places.

THE GIFT HORSE

The Protagonist gets what they want but not what they really needed

Getting what we want can be the most driving force we experience. Part of being human is to feel desire and to pursue those desires to varying degrees. While some hope their desires are eventually presented to them, without much effort, others go to extreme measures in order to grasp that which they long after. The problem with these pursuits is that they can feel empty when finally obtained. When what we want is not what we really need, the victory of the moment is robbed from us. In *Peppermint*, Riley North gets the revenge she so desperately desires from those who took that which she loved most in the world. However, what she needs is impossible to obtain, leaving her in deep pain even after she's accomplished her goal.

THE GREEK TRAGEDY

The protagonist gets neither what they wanted or needed

Perhaps the most difficult ending to execute is where the protagonist cannot get the satisfaction of their desires nor the inner fulfillment they truly need. These endings remain challenging because audiences have historically avoided such narratives, as they can be depressing and void of the hope we have come to expect in American storytelling. The theme of narratives that employ this type of irony is that sometimes we cannot have what we want in life, nor are we able to have what might bring us peace. In *Brokeback Mountain*, Ennis wants Jack as both a lover and a friend. He needs a life filled with romance, love, and acceptance. When he finds out Jack has been killed near the end of the story, both what he wants and needs are taken from him.

THE HOMERUN

The Protagonist gets both what they wanted and what they needed

It is rare in life that we get both what we want and what we need, make this ending the ultimate in irony. The challenge in crafting stories that will eventually end this way is to take the audience on a journey where they believe this ending won't be possible. Tragic twists and turns are required to lead the audience through a path filled with close calls and near misses in order to have the ultimate happiness befall the protagonist in the story's final moments. In *Sierra Burgess is a Loser*, the protagonist must endure losing both everything she wants and everything she needs before finally having both return to her in the narrative's final turn.

John Bucher

THE IRONIC EXERCISE

Select three stories you have created in the past. Look closely at how the stories ended. Determine if and when you chose any of the ironic endings discussed above. Would any of these endings have, perhaps, made for a better ending to your story?

WEEK 45

THE GRAND FINALE: APPROACHES TO TACKLING YOUR ENDING

A great deal of ink has been spilled about endings – in life, in all things we begin, and certainly in storytelling. Most of us are interested in finishing well. But how does one accomplish such a thing with a story? An entire volume could be written about the connection between a good *ending* and a good *beginning*, but that's for another time. For now, here are a few approaches to tackling the ending of your story with grace and finesse. Keep in mind, each approach will depend on the particulars of your script and the genre you are working in.

THE DIRECT APPROACH

Sometimes, there's no better way to end things than to give the audience exactly what they've been waiting for. Direct combat between the protagonist and antagonistic forces is a must when working in the genres of horror, sports stories, adventure, or war epics. In the final act of *Sully*, we see our hero pilot go head to head with forces hell-bent on questioning his judgement and ruining his reputation. The *James Bond* franchise ends nearly every one of their stories with this approach. *Friday Night Lights* and *Rocky* have memorable conclusions as a result of using the same tactic. *Hell or High Water, Silence of the Lambs* and *Alien* all put their protagonists in a mortal battle with their enemies in the end.

THE REVELATION APPROACH

The great reveal can be one of the most satisfying yet tricky endings to pull off in all of storytelling. It's only successful when the audience is given enough information that they should have seen the revelation coming, yet not so much that they have already guessed what the revelation is. The genres of mystery, thriller, and suspense all usually supply plenty of revelatory third acts. M. Night Shyamalan is perhaps the most beloved and hated of the third acts revelators. *The Sixth Sense*, *Unbreakable*, and *The Village* shocked, enchanted, and disappointed different fans with their third acts reveals. Edward Norton's revelation at the end of *Primal Fear* boosted his career to new levels. The reveals in the final moments of *Chinatown*, *Fight Club*, and *The Usual Suspects* have become iconic moments in our culture. *The Truman Show* and *Spotlight* both contain end reveals that were subtler but still greatly effective.

THE APPLICATION APPROACH

A character's arc is often verbalized in a story by talking about what they've learned over the course of the tale. Most films don't do this as directly as Dorothy's monologue does in the third act of *The Wizard of Oz*. However, the approach is still often used and highly effective. Seeing a character apply what they've learned (which is usually the theme of the story) can warm an audience's heart and even bring them to tears. This third act approach is consistently found in the comedy genre. *Shallow Hal*, *Liar Liar*, and *Bruce Almighty* are all examples. However, dramas also use this approach to great effect. *8 Mile*,

The Wolf of Wall Street, and *Stand By Me* all feature final acts where characters apply what they have learned over the course of the narrative. Perhaps the reason this approach works so well is its wide range of applications. *Groundhog Day* uses it. *Catch Me If You Can* does as well. And *The King's Speech* won Oscar gold with this approach.

THE AFTERMATH APPROACH

This is a more advanced technique where they audience is given a dénouement at the end of the third act. Stories exploring the aftermath of a given climax, must first have a climax worth exploring. The aftermath is often the cherry on top of the sundae. For example, after the dramatic climax in *Raiders of the Lost Ark*, we still have a scene where we see Indiana Jones frustrated with the results of the story and even a final moment where we are privy to the fate of the ark. In the *Shawshank Redemption*, we see the reuniting of the two main characters after Andy's climactic escape. *The Green Mile, Schindler's List, Back to the Future*, and *Good Will Hunting* all contain powerful scenes at the end of their third acts that have stuck in the memory of their audiences for years after the credits rolled.

THE GRAND FINALE EXERCISE

List the last three movies you watched or books you read. Make note of how each ended. Can you identify which (if any) ending listed above was used?

WEEK 46

WOUNDED HEALERS

Psychologist, Carl Jung popularized a term he assigned to fellow analysts that he observed had a desire to heal others, because they themselves were wounded in some way. He called these individuals *wounded healers*. This archetype has appeared time and again throughout storytelling as well. The Greek myth of Chiron tells of centaur who spent a great deal of his time assisting others with help and wise advice, despite being shot by one of Hercules arrows and incurably poisoned. Arthurian Legends speak of the Fisher King who was charged with keeping the Holy Grail despite being wounded in a way that prevented him from fathering the next generation that might take up his task after his death. And of course, television's Dr. House embodies both physical and emotional scars that are both his Achilles Heel and his motivation to help others. These characters offer an image of how many of us see our own inner lives – broken in many ways but still desiring to make the lives of others better. Here are possible ways to use wounded healers to enrich your story.

THE SELF DESTRUCTOR

Many of us have had people in our lives that seem bent on welcoming conflict and difficulty in their own journeys, despite being the most kind and helpful creatures one could ever hope to meet. The Self Destructor reflects the challenges that we face that we just can't seem to ever get past, no matter how many times we try. A doctor keeps a young gangster from dying of tuberculosis and convinces him to curb his own self-destruction all while battling his own severe alcoholism in Akira Kurosawa's *Drunken Angel*. This archetypal character is often used to bring out the best in another character while running their own train off the tracks. Jack is a wounded and self-destructive healer in *A Star is Born*.

THE SIN EATER

Some wounded characters bring healing to others through their own self-sacrifice. In a variety of traditions throughout history, sin eaters would consume a ritual meal in order to magically take on the sins of someone in their community or in some cases, and entire household, relieving them of any consequences of their actions. From the mythological Aztec goddess of earth, Tlazolteotl, to Jesus Christ -- those willing to take on the mistakes and wickedness of others have long been heroic figures in our stories, especially when those figures have endured great suffering themselves. Mike McDermott is a sin eater that takes on the debts of his despicable friend, Worm, in *Rounders*.

THE EMBODIED WOUND

While many Healer's wounds are psychological and emotional, others carry their wounds in their bodies. While these physical wounds most often metaphorically represent something greater than a mere carnal condition, the Healer that carries their challenges in a way that all the world can see affects the audience in a very different way than those with wounded psyches. For example, Eli's blindness offers as powerful irony for his Healer character in *The Book of Eli*. The Wounded Healer's embodiment often offers an opportunity to explore internal issues in very external and visual ways.

THE HIDDEN WOUND

Many characters are very in touch with their own wounds. They know how they are affected by their pain. Other characters hide their injuries behind humor, soft-hearted kindness, or even violently aggressive meanness. Hidden wounds may be invisible to the character who carries them, but at least one of the other characters in the story should be able to see them well. The writers of *Better Call Saul* used multiple seasons of their story to slowly demonstrate the impact of the Jimmy McGill's brother on his life, as well as the showing us the meaning behind the wounds he will carry long after his brother's death. Hidden wounds will eventually be brought to the surface at inopportune times in well-crafted stories.

THE CULTURAL WOUND

A Healer's task is lofty even when it is only a single person that needs help. However, when it's an entire culture or institution that needs healing, a Healer's wound can be overwhelming. In *The Handmaid's Tale*, June Osborne not only must carry her own painful hurts, she is also tasked with trying to heal an entire broken system. To make matters worse, the system she is up against does not want to be healed. Starr faces a similar struggle in *The Hate U Give*. Her character is scarred by what she has witnessed, but must overcome her wound in order to bring healing to the larger community. Cultural wounds often take a long time to produce even the smallest amount of healing. It is essential that you give your character enough time to believably affect change in their environment, which is often why these tasks are better suited to feature films or multiple seasons of television that shorter forms of storytelling.

THE WOUNDED HEALER EXERCISE

Examine the protagonist of a story you are creating or desire to create. Could this protagonist be a wounded healer? Write two to three paragraphs about how the character might embody this archetype.

WEEK 47

WORDS YOU SHOULD THINK TWICE BEFORE USING IN YOUR PERIOD STORY

Etymology is the study of the history of words. It's something surprisingly few storytellers know much about, considering that words are mostly what we actually have to work with. However, knowing where a word originated and the era it came out of can be of much use in telling truthful stories. If you ever write tales that took place in any decade before the one you were born in, you might be unaware that certain words and phrases didn't even exist in the time period you are crafting your story in. Sometimes, understanding the history behind a word or phrase actually provides a great deal of insight into how and why people said such things. For example, did you know that the word *mortgage* actually comes from the French *mort-gage* that literally means "death pledge?" Tragedy comes from the Greek word *tragodia*, which means *song of the male goat*, telling us something about the originator's opinion of certain Greek dramas. Here are several other words that you might reconsider using if you are writing a period piece in a specific era.

OK

There are a number of stories about the etymology of the word "ok." The most reliable is that that it dates back to 1839, when the *Boston Morning Post* began using the term as an editorial joke that went viral. If your story takes place before 1839, follow Léon's instructions to Mathilda in *The Professional* and "Stop saying ok all the time." Ok?

JUMBO

Some claim this word originated from the Swahili words *jambo* which means hello and *jumbe* which means chief. The term as we know it originated in 1860 in a London Zoo, where an elephant took on the name. P.T. Barnum later bought the elephant and brought him to international acclaim, propelling the word into our lexicon. The Disney film *Dumbo* is partially inspired by the real life Jumbo, who died in 1885. Everyone knows what the term means now, but if your story pre-dates 1860, no one would have had a clue.

QUARANTINE

Originating around 1520, the word is derived from the Latin *quardraginta*, literally meaning 40, and referred to the number of days a widow had the right to remain in her dead husband's house. In the 1660s, a similar Italian phrase *quarantine giorni*, which meant the span of 40 days, referred to the period a ship suspected of carrying a disease had to remain in the harbor before docking. A decade later the term took on the more general meaning of any period of forced isolation, which was hundreds of years before Ripley warned us about breaking quarantine in *Alien* or COVD-19.

LOOPHOLE

From the mid-15th century, the word referred to an opening in stone walls for shooting arrows through or admitting light. In the 1660s, the term became more generalized as a means of escape and later developed into the even more common idea about any ambiguity in a system, much like the one Ben Affleck and Matt Damon search for in *Dogma*.

NOON

Referencing time in a period film can be tricky business. We have only mostly agreed on a calendar system for roughly two centuries. Before this, most cultures had their own unique ways of tracking time. Our term *noon* comes from the Latin phrase *nona hora*, which literally means ninth hour. In ancient Rome, noon was around 3 PM, which might be why you never heard Russell Crowe referencing the time in *Gladiator*.

BUCK

Our common parlance for money didn't exist until American frontiersmen beginning using deerskins as units of commerce in the 19th century. Trading the bloody skins was likely as grotesque as Penny being sold to Humble Pie for 50 bucks and a case of beer in *Almost Famous*.

CLUE

In Greek mythology, when Theseus entered the labyrinth to kill the minotaur, he unraveled a "clew" or ball of string, so he could find his way out. Our iteration of the word didn't come about until the mid-1500s when people began using the spelling we recognize. Take that Col. Mustard, in the library, with the candlestick.

BRAINWASH

Originally the word was a military term used during the Korean War, before we recently adopted it as a description of anyone forcing another person to think a certain way. A number of films set before the 1950s use the term incorrectly. *The Manchurian Candidate* is not one of them. Released in 1962, the film brought the word to the attention of popular culture.

PAPARAZZI

Our term for freelance photographers that stalk celebrities actually originated in a fairly recent film. Signor Paparazzo was a street photographer in the 1960 Fellini classic *La Dolce Vita*. The name is a nod to the dialectical Italian word *paparazzo*, a buzzing insect.

DINOSAUR

From the Greek meaning "terrible lizard," the term is a relatively new one and was first coined by Sir Richard Owen in 1841, but still more than 150 years before *Jurassic Park* would be released.

DOLL

The word denoted a mistress in the 16th century and became a nickname for girls named Dorothy years later, before referring to a toy baby in the late 17th century. In 1955, the term again shifted its most common cultural meaning with the Marlon Brando film *Guys and Dolls*.

FUN

Originally meaning a trick, hoax, or practical joke, it was not until the 18th century that the word came to take on its present idea of amusement. So, if you're writing the next *Braveheart* or

300, remember that no one had *fun*.

THE WORD EXERCISE

Do your own research to find ten more words that would not be appropriate for a story set before the year 1900.

WEEK 48

WORKS OF LITERATURE THAT CAN IMPROVE YOUR STORYTELLING

It is unfortunate that many storyteller's familiarity with the classics of literature come only from the adaptations that have been made into films. While these movies sometimes become their own works of art, other times they simply don't hold up to the original written work. This has caused some creators to avoid reading the classic books that these films were based on. Seeing how masterful writers have put stories into words, executed themes, and developed characters can be of tremendous benefit when you are working on your own story. If you haven't read a classic work of literature since high school, perhaps it's time you visited your local library and took home a few books that might just take your storytelling to the next level. Here are a few important works of literature to consider picking up and how they can improve your writing.

Don Quixote by Miguel de Cervantes Saavedra (1615)

In this Spanish novel about a nobleman that sets out to revive chivalry and bring justice to the world, sidekick characters, such as Sancho Panza, serve as tremendous examples of how to use secondary characters to develop the story's protagonist. Any storyteller that works in the realm of fantasy or epics should make this important book required reading.

Frankenstein or, The Modern Prometheus by Mary Shelley (1818)

Infused with style from the Gothic and Romantic movements, Shelley creates an intense mood through her descriptions of atmosphere and environment. She mentally paints canvases in our mind where the stories she describes take place. Rich themes and layered characters fill the pages of the book, but audiences are left with nuanced and complex feelings as a result of the world that Shelley has created. Horror storytellers down to those who enjoy tackling social metaphors can find important examples of how to skillfully implement their ideas in this classic work.

Moby-Dick by Herman Melville (1851)

A masterful example of how a narrator, in this case a sailor named Ishmael, can paint a picture for the audience that could never be achieved in any other fashion. Through Ishmael, we come to understand the obsessive Captain Ahab, who seeks revenge on the white whale responsible for biting off his leg. We understand deep psychological themes of human nature in many of the lesser characters as well. Most of all, we are given a narrator whose voiceover brings us to deeper levels *within* the story, as opposed to simply lazily describing the scenery.

Their Eyes Were Watching God by Zora Neale Hurston (1937)

Coming of age stories have become a critical part of our current storytelling landscape. Every year, a great number of books, films, and TV shows center around this universal human experience. Hurston methodically walks us through the development of Janie Crawford, who journeys from being a teenage girl without a voice to a woman controlling the direction of her future. Hurston's attention to detail is worth aspiring to.

Native Son by Richard Wright (1940)

In this story of a man called Bigger Thomas, issues of race, crime, and poverty are explored with a raw yet poetic intensity. Writers who wish to deal with the realities of urban life, the difficulties of justice in America, and the importance of social protest will find help in examining how Wright executes his vision for the soul of the country.

Wise Blood by Flannery O'Conner (1952)

The story of a WWII vet who returns home to his eccentric Southern town and starts an anti-religious ministry, *Wise Blood* examines the crises of faith that many people face when life becomes more complicated than the dogma of their youth allows for. Storytellers that deal with the challenges and wonder of spirituality would do well to examine how O'Conner tackles such weighty issues, as her approach feels timeless and always relevant.

Ficciones (Fictions) by Jorge Luis Borges (1962)

A collection of short stories, Borges most celebrated work offers different storytelling lessons in every narrative. Storytellers that commonly work with philosophical issues, secret societies, and conspiracies should familiarize themselves with how this legendary writer executes realism with that which exists within the human mind and consciousness.

Beloved by Toni Morrison (1987)

Set after the Civil War, *Beloved* is a fine example of the American epic. Inspired by the story of Margaret Garner, a woman who escaped slavery to the free states, Morrison takes real life events and fictionalizes them with amazing results. Any storyteller wishing to take events from history and turn them into scripted narratives can learn a great deal from looking at *Beloved.*

A Wild Sheep Chase by Haruki Murakami (1989)

A detective story focused around an unnamed chain-smoking narrator, the book uses allegory like few others in our modern era. Murakami uses specifics of Japanese middle class culture that resonate with American middle class culture in an effort to make his storytelling universal. Storytellers wishing to tell a genre story outside their own culture owe it to themselves to read Murakami's work.

THE LITERATURE EXERCISE

Select one book from the current *New York Times Best Seller List* and commit to begin reading it this week.

WEEK 49

HOW TO RESURRECT AN OLD STORY

It's seldom discussed, but most storytellers must get a lot of bad narratives out before any solid storytelling begins flowing from us. As we grow, we see our own development and tend to discard the stories we worked on earlier in our journey. While our style may have left much to be desired, it doesn't mean that there were not some gold nuggets in the midst of the carnage we rightfully discarded. Some of our best ideas may have emerged before we started *thinking* too much about our storytelling. Before you burn old stories or cast them into the outer reaches of your hard drive, make sure there are not elements you want to save for later when your storytelling has matured. If you've been crafting stories for a while, go back and look at some of your early work. Are there ideas that still hold charge for you? Here are ways to avoid throwing out the baby with the bathwater.

RESURRECT THE CHARACTER

Perhaps you had created a fascinating character but just didn't know what to do with her. Perhaps she represented a large part of who you were at that time in your life. Characters can embody truth that transcends description and words. Your character might still feel like someone you want to explore and live with for a while. Developing a strong character can be one of the most difficult things to accomplish in all of storytelling. If you were able to do that but just couldn't find a journey that worked, reviving that character later, after you've developed better plotting skills, can lead to powerful storytelling. Remember *Wonder Woman* scripts floated around Hollywood for a long time before someone was able to execute a plot worthy of such a powerful character.

RESURRECT THE PLOT

Did you know that the plot of *Die Hard* was written as a sequel for Arnold Schwarzenegger's *Commando*? Or that *Oceans 12* was originally developed as a project called *Honor Among Thieves* before having its plot brought over to the successful Soderberg franchise? Sometimes, we have a great idea for a story but our characters aren't the best fit for the narrative we are constructing. This could have been the case with some of your early stories. Most of us can recognize when we stumble on a simple yet effective plotline to build a story around. The magic occurs when we are then able to execute that plot with characters that keep the audience interested in the story. Even if an entire plot is not workable, there may be elements of that can be salvaged from a story that was discarded long ago.

RESURRECT THE CONCEPT

Your characters may have been flat. Your plot may have been overly complex and confusing. However, that doesn't mean that the original concept for the story you were crafting wasn't worth developing. Our abilities at executing a story usually get better the longer we work at it. It's quite possible that you just didn't have the chops to tackle the killer idea you had in the early days of your storytelling career. Dusting off the concept, then adding fresh characters and a better structure to hang the plot on, might make all the difference. James Cameron had the concept for *Avatar* before he made *Titanic* but knew he didn't have the skill set or technology yet to accomplish his vision. Putting a story in a drawer for a while may not be a bad idea, as long as we remember to get it back out when we have developed the necessary abilities to pull it off.

THE RESSURECTION EXERCISE

Find an old story from your earliest days of storytelling. Write two to three paragraphs on how you could resurrect something from the discarded story into your current work.

WEEK 50

WHAT TO DO WHEN YOUR STORY IDEA IS TAKEN BY SOMEONE ELSE

If you tell stories for any length of time, eventually you will see an idea you had be successfully executed by someone else. The downside, of course, will be that you had no involvement with the project at all. It's enough to cause one to embrace conspiracy theories about Hollywood spies staking out coffee shops and combing through personal hard drives in search of Final Draft files. The odd truth is that ideas seem to float in the air at certain moments and multiple storytellers will grab them at the same time, confident that they have a unique idea.

I once saw the trailer for a film called *Professor Marston and the Wonder Women*. It is based on the true story of William Moulton Marston and how he created the comic character of Wonder Woman while balancing a polyamorous relationship with two women. I had been developing a script called *The Wonder Man*, based on the exact same premise. I stumbled on Marston's story a few years before there was even talk of a *Wonder Woman* film, much less a project around Marston's life. I worked hard to develop research around the project. I banged out an outline. I even had concept poster art created to empower my pitch as I took it around Hollywood. I spent grueling hours writing the script, trying to get it polished after

I heard rumors of a *Wonder Woman* film in development from Warner Bros. I knew if I had my project ready at the right moment, there would be interest around Marston and who he was. And I was right. Unfortunately, there were others who had stumbled on Marston's story as well. They had gone through the same process I had and one of them managed to sell their story and see the film made before I did.

This wasn't the first time I had this experience. I had been plotting out an NWA biopic for more than five years before *Straight Outta Compton* was announced. I was shopping a comedy about a man in a dead-end job who fakes his own death several years before Adam's Sandler's *Do-Over* was created. And the list goes on and on. Had storytellers somehow divined what I was working on, stole it, and beat me to market? No. They saw the same idea floating around in the air and grabbed it. They did beat me to the market, but this is where the many adages in Hollywood about luck come into play. So, what does a storyteller do when the idea you've been working on hits the big screen at a theater near you, or even worse, becomes the next binge-worthy hit on Netflix? Here are three ways to move forward when you find out your story has been snatched.

REMIX IT

Your story might still be salvageable. Depending on how close your premise is to the one that has been produced, you might be able to change key elements of the story to make it workable. For example, significant changes to who the protagonist is might make the story feel very different. If your hero was a Korean businessman in the cutthroat world of advertising, pivoting to an African American woman in the competitive world of on-line startups would likely make the script so different, that your story can have new life again. Of course, this will require a significant amount of work. However, it might allow you to still keep important sections of your script, including setups and payoffs, killer dialogue, and plot twists. Another common remixing technique is to set your story in a different historical era than you've been working in. If your script about a lawyer who falls in love with her criminal client shows up in the "Coming Soon" trailers on HBO, consider taking your story 100 years into the future. Shifting to a different moment in history gives stories a new context that removes obvious similarities when being compared to stories that have already been produced.

BURY IT

While it requires patience, sometimes putting a story in your desk drawer is the best career move you can make. The film that stole your idea might go by relatively unnoticed at the box office. In a few years, it's completely possible that few will even remember it was made. There could be renewed interest in your script. Many historical figures and events have had numerous films made about them, some even within a few months of each other. This can be an especially helpful strategy when your take on the material is through a significantly different lens, though the subject itself is being given the current spotlight. Reboots of material have become a standard and the period between reboots has gotten shorter and shorter, thanks to our friends working in the superhero genre. Just because the film about vampire high school students just snatched your premise and tanked at the box office does not mean that Hollywood won't be ready to try that idea again in a few years. Hold on to your story. Its time may still be yet to come.

BURN IT

Sometimes, a narrative is so similar that the only option is to send it to that old story farm where stories go to die. My NWA script lives there now. *Straight Outta Compton* was well done, successful, and crafted by those who experienced the story in real life. It is highly unlikely anyone will be looking for my take on that material in the future. It would be a waste of time to continue trying to make anything of the script. This should always be a last resort, but an option that every storyteller is willing to take for their own sanity. Most commonly, this happens with historical biopics and stories based around a singular event from history. Before abandoning an idea completely, make sure that it cannot be remixed, or shouldn't instead be buried, as discussed above. If there are simply no better options, move on to developing other projects in building your arsenal of stories. Having a wide repertoire of stories is the most effective way to avoid stalling your career when a great idea gets snatched.

THE SNATCHED EXERCISE

Find two films about the same event or character. Watch both. Write two to three paragraphs about how each creator approached and executed the story differently.

WEEK 51

THE 7 DAY CHARACTER PRIMER

Having taught and lectured on story for more than fifteen years, I have come to the conviction that character is usually the best place to start when beginning the process of crafting a story. A trend that I've noticed that past few years with many new creators is the tendency to rush through the character process in order to quickly get to the fascinating concept that their story is based around. Sometimes, a storyteller is halfway through creating their story before their protagonist has an occupation, a backstory, or even a name. While it is not *required* that you begin with a character before developing your concept, the character work really *should* be done at some point in your process. Beginning with a solid human base (even if your character isn't human) can make characters, and thus their stories, feel more real. One of the deepest philosophical ideas we confront when we tell stories is what it means to be human. Wrapping our characters in detailed flesh when creating a story is one of the surest ways to give the story believability, emotional resonance, and nuance. Here is a seven-day primer to get your character ready for your storytelling journey.

DAY ONE – GIVE THEM A NAME

Some storytellers flippantly choose a name for their character off the top of their head. Other writers methodically craft a name with layers of meaning. The *Alien* Franchise has often relied on one-word names for their characters, like Daniels or Ripley. Sometimes simple one-syllable first and last names, like Rick Blaine in *Casablanca*, speak to the hard edge the character embodies. Other times, playful names, like Verbal Kint, in *The Usual Suspects* seem to hint at the characteristics of a character. Regardless of what works best for your story, actually think about the name of your protagonist. Why does this name you have given her or him best suit them? One of the first things we learn about someone when we first meet them is their name. This is helpful when meeting our characters too.

DAY TWO – GIVE THEM A JOB

Even if this detail is unrelated to the story you are telling, as may be the case in a horror film or romantic comedy, establishing this in your own mind, as the storyteller, is important to making the character feel real. Remember, being a student or a parent is just as much of a job as being a doctor or lawyer. Captain Jack Sparrow, in the *Pirates of the Caribbean* franchise, captains ships. Louise Banks is a linguistics professor in *Arrival*. Mia Dolan is a barista in *La La Land*. All loosely connect to the story they are a part of, but are details that flesh out who these characters are.

DAY THREE – GIVE THEM A QUIRK

Quirks come in many forms. While we usually think of them in terms of an odd habit, like collecting heavily used forks from thrift stores, there are a number of different ways to make your character uniquely human. Giving the protagonist a unique external flaw, either in appearance or behavior, is one method, especially when that flaw speaks to an inner need. Giving the character a "ghost" from their past that haunts their present is another. Quirks don't have to be dark either. Having a character constantly chomping on Flintstone vitamins is funny as we all can relate to their chewy tastiness, but also speaks to the character's metaphorical desire for health. Peter Quill's penchant for 80s music in *Guardians of the Galaxy* is fun, but also speaks to his connection to his dead mother. Jimmy McGill seems to enjoy amateur video production, which speaks to his desperation to be known at any cost, on *Better Call Saul.* Sheldon Cooper is a character built almost completely around quirks on *The Big Bang Theory.*

DAY FOUR – GIVE THEM SOMETHING TO LOVE

What a character loves can be a person, place, or thing. It can even be a feeling or an idea. Many of the most impactful characters have been those that loved *themselves* above all else. What your character loves will likely be connected to some sort of sacrifice they should be challenged to make in your story. The protagonist may or may not decide to give up what they love, but they should be forced into making that decision at some point. Celeste Wright is forced to sacrifice the comfortable life she loves in order to protect herself and her children in *Big Little Lies*. In *Manchester By the Sea*, Lee Chandler gives up the independence he loves, for something he loves more – family. In *Going in Style*, the main characters go to even greater lengths for the ones the love. Using family in general, or a specific family member, can be a powerful force of love to give your character, as love of family is a universally-understood motivator.

DAY FIVE – GIVE THEM SOMETHING TO HATE

Knowing what your character despises can be as powerful as knowing what they hate. This also may take the form of a person, place, thing, or more abstract idea. What your character hates will likely come into contact with what she loves, driving her to action. In *Logan,* our protagonist's love and concern for himself is outweighed by his hate of injustice. Amy hates what she believes is the unrealistic expectation of monogamy in *Trainwreck.* In *Rogue One,* Jyn Erso must confront her hate for Orson Krennic, the man responsible for the death of her mother.

DAY SIX – GIVE THEM A WANT

Knowing what a character wants and why they want it is perhaps the most interesting thing we can reveal about any character. Desire and motivation are two of the most core principles that we relate to as humans. The earlier your audience understand what your character wants and why they want it, the faster their engagement will be. Determining this early on in your character development and story process saves hours of meandering later. Greg desperately wants to get to a video game convention instead of Meemaw's 90th birthday celebration in *Diary of a Wimpy Kid: The Long Haul.* In *Boss Baby*, our protagonist wants to put a stop to the plot of the CEO of Puppy Co. Maximo wants true love, after having made a career of seducing women, in *How to be a Latin Lover.*

DAY SEVEN – GIVE THEM A NEED

Often times, what a character needs is more important than what they want. Your character may or may not be aware of what he or she needs, but as the writer we must know. In most genres, the protagonist gets what they need, regardless of whether they get what they want. However, this is not always the case. Knowing up front what it is that your character truly needs can help as you begin crafting an outline for the span of the story, and especially how it will end. *Bridget Jones* often pines after one man, when the other is who she truly needs. In *Chuck*, the protagonist wants success as a boxer, but he needs to accept himself. Chris wants to make things work with his girlfriend and her parents, but what he needs is to *Get Out*, as the title suggests.

THE CHARACTER EXERCISE

Create a character around the seven ideas outlined above.

WEEK 52

SIX WRITING EXERCISES YOU CAN DO IN SIXTY SECONDS OR LESS

Time – It is the feared enemy of the storyteller. If time was not an issue, many of us would have churned out thousands of stories by now. Time often assures that we never ever actually *practice* our craft. We cannot imagine a musician who never practices scales. We would never expect a painter who never practices to one day become Picasso. So why do we assume the next *Wizard of Oz* will one day just find its way into our story arsenal without practice? We don't practice because we usually simply don't have the time. Here are six storytelling exercises, named after the characters that inspired them, that you can squeeze into your schedule in sixty seconds or less.

THE NEGAN

What is your character's biggest secret? Who knows and who doesn't? Perhaps it is only a secret to the audience, such as who Negan killed on *The Walking Dead*. Write for one minute about a juicy secret a character could hold.

THE HANNIBAL LECTOR

Spend sixty seconds coming up with as many adjectives for an antagonist as you can. Don't think too hard about any single word, just let as many flow out as possible.

THE ERIN BROCKOVICH

Decide on two (or three if you have time) "ghosts" or wounds from a potential character's backstory that would inform their life.

THE BRIDGET JONES

Come up with one difficult decision that would force a character to choose between two amazing options or two horrible options.

THE MARTY MCFLY

Spend sixty seconds writing about how your character gets around from place to place and what that says about them. HINT: For Marty McFly in *Back to the Future*, it was a skateboard.

THE JUNO MACGUFF

Write about a type of character whose story you have never seen on-screen before. If you have time, describe why they are difficult to execute.

SEASONS 1

TO EVERYTHING THERE IS A SEASON: A STORY FOR EVERY SEASON

There are many calendars in the world of storytelling. Here are ways to use the seasons to create a story you're crafting any time of the year.

SUMMER STORIES

Summer is often associated with a time when people vacation, both physically and mentally. If we are going to take a chance or do something risky, chances are we will do it in the summer so we can "put things back together" in the more respectable fall season. In stories that take place in school settings, summer represents the deadline of all deadlines. Characters must tell their crushes how they feel before they don't see them again until autumn. In many high school stories, summertime can be a season for reinvention. *Grease* is a perfect example of a story where characters are grappling with all that took place over the summer. Films where a protagonist will reinvent themselves often begin with a physical graduation at the end of the school year and then end with a metaphoric graduation in their life. *The Sisterhood of the Traveling Pants* takes place over a summer. *The Great Gatsby*, *To Kill A Mockingbird*, and *A Walk to Remember* and *Jaws* do as well. Spike Lee's *Do The*

Right Thing takes place on a single day during the hottest summer on record in New York. The heat we experience during this season can play as a metaphor for the tension a character experiences, the passion they feel, or thawing that occurs in their soul.

FALL/AUTUMN STORIES

Autumn is perhaps the most ignored season. Summer has faded and winter has yet to arrive. However, autumn doesn't carry the hope that spring does and therefore often gets left out of seasonal discussions. Like the leaves that change their color, autumn can be a time when a character "goes to the underworld" or experiences a death of some sort. Difficult transitions are what autumn is all about. Most horror films take place in the fall, likely because of the proximity to Halloween. Stories about football often take place in this season for similar reasons. *E.T.*, *Dead Poets Society*, *Stepmom*, *Rushmore*, and *St. Elmo's Fire* all mostly take place in the fall. *Good Will Hunting*, *Garden State*, and *American Beauty* do as well.

Just because a story takes place in autumn doesn't mean it has to end unhappily, however. *When Harry Met Sally*, *The Straight Story*, and *Dan in Real Life* all take place in this season. If your story is about great transition, fall might be a perfect setting for the journey your characters are undertaking.

WINTER STORIES

Winter stories can serve a wide variety of purposes. The bitter cold can symbolize the isolation one feels after a death or break up. The snow can represent the worst of obstacles or the beauty of life. Ice can be a challenge to be overcome or the setting for romance when frozen lakes and ice skates are involved. Of course, Christmas movies are set in the winter --

when a character might experience the beautiful reflection of family or the humor of odd relatives. The season is romantic in *A Winter's Tale*. It's adventurous in *The Call of the Wild*. It's hilarious in *Christmas Vacation*. It jerks tears in *Love Actually*. And it's horrifying in *Misery* and *The Shinning*. You might call winter the Swiss Army Knife of storytelling.

SPRING STORIES

Spring stories are usually about rebirth. Flowers bloom. Trees blossom. Animals mate. Love is in the air. The death of winter is behind us and it's time to begin again. It's enough to make one want to sing. Which could be why musicals like *State Fair*, *Meet Me in St. Louis* and *Seven Brides For Seven Brothers* are all set in spring. Baseball films like *Moneyball* usually take place in the season. We mustn't forget that spring break is also in the spring, which lends a moment of hedonism to some characters as in *Spring Breakers* and *Where the Boys Are. Emma* and *The Secret Garden* celebrate the carefree aspects of the season. Some stories take advantage of the logistics of spring, such as *Rear Window*, where everyone has their windows open, allowing for the plot to move forward. Spring-themed stories also play well outside the United States. Check out *The Adventures of Reinette and Mirablle*, and *Spring, Summer, Fall, Winter...and Spring* for examples. Using springtime as an element in your story takes advantage of a part of your audience's psyche they bring with them. They understand the metaphors and tropes associated with this season without you ever having to explain them, which makes for the most effective sort of storytelling.

SEASONS 2

SEASONS OF CHANGE: Secrets for Rebooting Your Story

Sometimes, stories need a significant shift in approach in order to relight the spark that gave them their start. Here are changes you can make to your story in order to help it take flight.

CHANGE THE TIME PERIOD

The romantic comedy you've been working on is fun but needs that extra something. Have you thought about setting it in the Wild West? Medieval London? The year 2099? *The Nice Guys* took an average buddy cop concept and gave it the style of the 1970s. *The Diary of A Teenage Girl* and *Everybody Wants Some* utilized the same time period but to much different effect. *Sing Street* would have worked fine as a modern tale but setting the film in the 1980s allowed the audience to bring their own nostalgia to the story. Setting *The Lobster* in the future allowed the storytellers to remove any objections from our mind that we might have about the premise of the story. *Loving* and *Rules Don't Apply* both are set in earlier decades as they are loosely based on historical events. However, both stories use the time period as a pseudo-character in the film, helping the audience to better understand the internal journeys of their protagonists.

CHANGE THE LOCALE

Do stories set in New York differ from those set in Texas? Do stories in the mountains differ from those set in the desert? Do stories set in the woods differ from those set in a submarine? The answer is, of course, a resounding yes. The setting and locale of a story affects everything from the narrative tone to the way that characters to relate the environments around them. *Green Room* could have been set in a seedy punk club in East Greenwich Village but setting it in an underground venue deep in the forest of the Pacific Northwest adds a level of mystery to the story that might not be there otherwise. *Moonlight* could take place most anywhere. However, setting it near the ocean provided literal and metaphoric waves and beaches that added additional layers to the character development and unfolding narrative.

CHANGE THE PROTAGONIST'S AGE, RACE, OR GENDER

When developing a story, one of the simplest yet helpful questions that you can ask involves changing the protagonist's most basic identity. That story of a young woman dating outside her race becomes radically different when her character shifts to an octogenarian in a nursing home. The story of a middle-aged man trying to win a karate championship is nice but becomes more interesting when the story shifts around a middle-aged woman. The story of young Irish men who came to America to make their way is not uncommon, but *Brooklyn* gave a new lens to see the story through – that of a young woman. *Raging Bull* and *Rocky* opened up the world of Italian boxers, but *Creed* told the story of a character we had not often seen before. *Sherlock Holmes* allowed us to see a young and virile Robert Downey Jr. in great action, but *Mr. Holmes* gives us deeper insight into who the character really is by showing us life reflected in his later years.

CHANGE THE GENRE

Few storytellers know that *Good Will Hunting* actually began as a sci-fi thriller. Among other things, the shift in genre made it an Oscar winner. Changing the genre of your story changes the structural rules. It changes what can be done with the characters and the possibilities with their external goals. For some time, seeing a woman struggle in the workplace made for serious dramas. *The Devil Wears Prada* and *Trainwreck* opened up new avenues for the story trope by moving the narrative to the comedy genre. *Shaft* and other stories from African American cinema in the 1970s told us stories of revenge and race, but *Django Unchained* moved the familiar tale to the western genre and gained an entirely new audience. Shifting the genre should fundamentally shift the story, not necessarily the external goal of the main character, but instead what the audience feels and experiences in it.

SEASONS 3

FOUR SEASONS OF LIFE TO DRAW STORY FROM

Some seasons in our life are more exciting than others. Many days come and go without a single notable event. The times that do stand out may be full of joy, great sadness, anxiety-inducing drama, or simple gratitude. When telling stories, we generally want to include a day or term of the protagonist's life that is unusual or noteworthy. While our story may begin on an ordinary day, life's circumstances should bring about something that is out of the norm or the main character's reaction to the norm should change. Finding seasons of life that are rich in opportunity for your script can mean the difference between a page-turner and the narrative doldrums. Here are four seasons of life to consider drawing your story out of.

SEASONS OF CHANGE

Change is one of the only certainties we have in life. It is the instigator of both great hope and crippling dread. Passing through thresholds and rites of initiation are universal experiences that people relate to, regardless of time and geography. Marriage, divorce, births, and deaths are times of change that hold moments ripe for story. Coming of age tales set in schools lend themselves to narrative elements, as there is always conflict, a ticking clock toward the end of the school year, and ceremonial rites such as graduation, proms, dances, and moving to the next grade. Bo Burnham's *Eight Grade* exemplifies the seasons of change one experiences in moving from middle school to high school. Physical changes, social changes, and changes in relationships are all at play during this period of life. While you may or may not have ever had the life experiences of a teen girl in middle school, the universal seasons of change she walks through apply to the particulars of many experiences.

SEASONS OF PAIN

Difficulties are nearly as universal as change. The degree of difficulty we experience may vary from person to person. However, few of us get through life without overcoming some obstacles. Whether we've ever experienced the specific pain we see a character undergo on screen rarely matters. We resonate with most all complications. Seeing characters traverse seasons of pain can also work across genres. In addition, we don't necessarily have to see the protagonist escape the pain they are experiencing, as long as they find some resolution within themselves to go on. Gus Van Sant's *Don't Worry, He Won't Get Far on Foot* explores the life of a character whose journey is full of pain and sadness. But it's the tenacity of the character throughout the season of pain we come to celebrate by the time the credits roll.

SEASONS OF INSIGHT

We've all had the moment where the cartoonish lightbulb appears above our head and we come to realize something that had never occurred to us before. While impossible to manufacture in our lives, we recognize the value of these moments when they do happen. Sometimes, we experience entire seasons of life where new insights seem to constantly be coming our way. Many times, these insights are the product of change, but other times there seems to be no clear catalyst for their appearance. Still other times, we reach internal milestones within ourselves where wisdom has been earned, achieved, and full realized. Seasons of insight often come as a result of old age or retirement. Others come as a result of having a child or losing a job. The most common season of insight comes after we've made a huge mistake in life. Perhaps we've foolishly left a relationship or put our trust in someone who let us down. The lessons we learn are valuable and precious as we pick ourselves up and walk forward. We often must choose between bitterness and stagnation or risking our pride to try again. In Brad Bird's *Incredibles 2*, Mr. Incredible experiences a season of insight when he mistakenly feels he has less worth while staying home to care of the kids while his wife is out saving the world. His journey with this experience teaches him a valuable lesson – one that we all enjoy being reminded of.

SEASONS OF THE UNEXPECTED

Some days we wake up and have no idea what awaits us before we go to bed again. It could be the opportunity of a lifetime or an event we've long feared. Painful moments and difficult change sometimes give us plenty of opportunity to prepare for them. A relative's long illness may offer the chance to say goodbye before they die. A family move that will force the kids to change schools may be impending until the end of the school year. However, some challenges strike completely out of the blue. We have no way to prepare for the unexpected. Characters in these situations are rich and intriguing to audiences. We are curious to see how they handle the unexpected, closely comparing their choices to the ones we would make. In Margaret Atwood's

The Handmaid's Tale, June Osbourne is constantly challenged because she is in a season of her life that she never saw coming. It descended on her quickly and without warning.

SEASONS 4

HANGING THE SUN, MOON, AND STARS: *Using Astronomical Symbols in Storytelling*

Many of the most impactful symbols in stories are ancient in origin. Using animals, plants, and trees to represent ideas, feelings, and seasons in the human experience is a practice that dates back to the earliest stories we have record of. There are perhaps no other elements used more often in these early stories than the celestial bodies people saw when they stared into the sky. Here are ways the sun, moon, and stars have been used in storytelling and what they have symbolically been used to represent.

THE SUN

Early peoples from a variety of different regions worshipped the sun and saw it as a representation of God, if not God itself. They created myths giving it the name Ra, or Apollo, or Amaterasu, depending on their mythological tradition. It has symbolized ultimate power, the ability to bring forth life, as with plants, and knowledge or revelation as it brings light. It has also symbolized the inevitable retribution for egos run amok, as with Icarus. In the upcoming *Adrift*, the sun symbolizes the hope for survival, breaking through the clouds, after a storm. In *Sunshine*, the death of the sun symbolizes the slow extinction of human consciousness. In *Nosferatu,* the sun represents the destruction of evil, a trope that would be used in countless vampire films that followed. Seeing the sun disappear in the sky, via a solar eclipse has also been mightily used across genres in films like *Fantasia,* where it was used dramatically through animation, *The Watcher in the Woods,* where it was used to create horror, and in *Little Shop of Horrors,* where it was used for comedic effect.

THE MOON

Where Apollo was represented by the sun in ancient mythology, his sister, Artemis, was represented by the moon, an equally meaningful feminine symbol for humanity. Not always a symbol of the feminine, one of the earliest and most iconic images in all of film is from Georges Méliès's *A Trip to the Moon,* where it symbolized humankind's most dramatic external goal, an idea that would become more nuanced yet still present in modern films like *Moon* and *Apollo 13.* The moon symbolized power and revenge when Gru decided to steal it right out of the sky in *Despicable Me.* It symbolized beauty as it washes over the skin of black men in *Moonlight.* A full moon brings out the worst in many characters, especially in films like *American Werewolf in London.* Elliot and *E.T.* ride past the moon, a symbol of the wonder they are both experiencing. The moon almost always symbolizes bad things just around the corner in the horror genre but more than one Disney character has shared a romantic moment silhouetted by that giant light in the night sky.

THE STARS

Similar to the moon, the stars can invoke the mystery or mysterious hope of the human experience, in the midst of darkness. The final moments of the first season of *True Detective* take place as the two main characters look up at the stars and offer one of the more powerful exchanges about the meaning of light and darkness that television has ever seen. Ryan Gosling and Emma Stone enjoy a fanciful dance through the stars, symbolizing both the multitude of artists trying to make it in Los Angeles and the hope that one might do just that in *La La Land*. *WALL-E* stares up at the stars, which symbolize that which is beyond what he knows – a trope used in stories ranging from *Star Trek* to *Pinocchio*. Falling stars have their own meaning as symbols in film. And sometimes, stars simply embody the desires of a character that wishes on them. They also often represent a final destination or home for characters after death as with the final tearful moments of *The Iron Giant*.

SEASONS 5

STORY LESSONS FROM CHRISTMAS MOVIES

Though America's customs have shifted and melded throughout the decades, and a number of different religious traditions are celebrated in mid and late December, only one has amassed such a number of films to establish its own genre. I'm referring, of course, to the Christmas movie. Wrapped presents, decorated trees, Nativity sets, stockings, home-cooked food, and perhaps even a visit from Santa Claus himself, are all tropes that create an environment of nostalgia and joy for many moviegoers. However, without a solid story behind them, these elements simply become archetypal window dressing. When done well, Christmas movies remind us of the reasons why this season has become so special to so many people. Here are story lessons we can take from Christmas movies.

FAMILY ISSUES ALWAYS MAKE GREAT STORIES

Examples: *Daddy's Home 2, National Lampoon's Christmas Vacation, A Christmas Story*

For many, Christmas involves travel, carrying packages, and seeing relatives that we only encounter once a year. There's a reason why we love to laugh at the difficult cousin that insists on talking politics at Christmas dinner – because so many of us have been there. The holiday season is a time when people express their love to the ones they're closest too, but when emotions are running so high, there's bound to be a few road blocks along the way. While conflict in families can work as a powerful tool in any film, finding an organic reason to put families in the same physical space can be challenging. Christmas is an ideal way to accomplish this, but certainly not the only way. Weddings, funerals, births, birthdays, anniversaries, and retirements are just a few ways you can force characters into the same room together.

WE ALL SOMETIMES FEEL LIKE FISH OUT OF WATER

Examples: *Elf, Rudolph the Red Nosed Reindeer, Frosty the Snowman*

The holidays are not a pleasant time for everyone. Some are confronted with the absence of family members who used to gather with them. Others are faced with their own loneliness. The emotions of the season can highlight what we don't have instead of those things we should be thankful for. Stories that remind us that we all feel out of place at different times can be of great comfort. Seeing a character that struggles to connect with those around them can both make us laugh and make us cry. These stories create a sense of empathy *within us* and give us hope that others may have empathy *for us*. Most powerfully, they can bring assurances that we are not alone.

MOMENTS OF REFLECTION ARE UNIVERSAL

Examples: *A Christmas Carol, Scrooged, It's A Wonderful Life*

The reflective holiday film has almost become a genre unto itself. There's a reason these films seem to resonate with audiences year after year. Our lives feel busier every year. Things never seem to slow down. It never becomes easy to find the time to process and contemplate the experiences we've had – and yet we all continue to recognize the importance of it. Seeing characters stop and smell the roses, be confronted with the unhealthy ways they are living, and decide to turn over a new leaf give us hope that perhaps we, too, are capable of doing so. As with family stories, we must give characters a reason to pause their lives. While the holidays can be a great excuse for this – an illness, the death of a loved one, and being fired from a job are all other motivating factors in stories that revolve around a character who ends up experiencing a reflection.

PITCHING 1

DIFFERENT APPROACHES TO PITCHING

Most storytellers don't enjoy the luxury of having top talent attached to their project when pitching. We have to rely on other strengths. While there is certain content that every pitch should have, writers still must choose where to lean in when pitching. Where you choose to focus your attention can make all the difference to a listener who stays engaged or one who immediately checks out. Here are different approaches to pitching your story, each highlighting a separate strategy to consider focusing on.

THE PERSONAL TOUCH

Having a personal connection to the material you are pitching is one of the strongest ways to hold the listener's interest. This doesn't mean that the story you are pitching needs to be based on your life. Any sort of connection that explains why you have passion for your project is helpful. If your protagonist is struggling with romance, giving a bit of insight into your own struggles can strike a connection. If your main character is fighting against the system, a connection about your own battles might prove worthy of a mention. And of course, if your character struggles with a rare disease that you have suffered with as well, be sure to mention that. Listeners are trying to identify why *you* are the perfect person to tell this story and understand your insights into its nuances. When Diablo Cody pitched *Juno*, she used her own life experiences of being a quirky outcast as a connection to the material. What qualities and experiences in your life might make your pitch more personal?

THE PRE-EXISTING INTEREST

Some stories already have a bit of built-in interest. Scripts that take place in a particular historical period or around a historical character (that no longer requires life rights) can produce immediate interest in a listener, if that period or character is one he or she is interested in. The same holds true for popular genres and material that bares resemblance to a property that has already proved successful but may be just out of the public's collective memory. Few of us will ever have the opportunity to pitch the next *Spiderman* story, but that doesn't mean we can't find material connected to interests that already exist. *King Arthur: Legend of the Sword* didn't fare so well at the box office, but it got made because there was a pre-existing interest in the material. Does your story connect to an interest that already has some sort of fan base? If so, it might mean greater chances for your project.

THE HIGH CONCEPT HOOK

Some pitches gain interest for no other reason than that they are simply a good idea that no one has made a project about before. These pitches often begin by asking "what if...?" What if there was a theme park filled with real dinosaurs? What if the man of your dreams became your roommate? What if a farm boy had an opportunity to save the galaxy? All these are examples of how asking "what if...?" can lead to a strong story and a strong pitch. *Fist Fight* asked what if a teacher at your high school challenged another teacher to a brawl. That simple one-sentence pitch brings a chuckle just to read. Our mind races with the possibilities for comedic humor. A great pitch gives the listeners just enough information that they begin writing moments for the story in their own head.

THE UNIVERSAL STORY

Some pitches connect because we can all relate the underlying story or theme. Universal stories provide a short cut to needing to explain plot intricacies. When a boy struggles to win the approval of his father – we understand. When a woman seeks to find her place in the world without relying on others – we understand. When characters take out on the open road, looking for adventure and meaning – we understand. Connecting your material to a universal desire or need that we all share is one sure way to make sure that a listener has some resonance with your story. What theme is reinforced in your script? Is that theme as universal to Kabul as it is to Kansas? A pitch for *Boss Baby* might go something like this. *Have you ever felt like someone has come along and undeservedly taken what you had worked so hard for? Have you ever felt like you're not seen? Tim sure does. His new baby brother is getting all the family's attention and he needs to find a solution.* While we only get a wink at the larger story in this pitch, we can all relate to Tim's plight. We've all been there. That's the exact feeling we want to create in the listener when they hear our pitch.

PITCHING 2

WORDS THAT WILL STRENGTHEN YOUR STORY'S PITCH

A listener will usually know in the first ten seconds of hearing about your story if their curiosity has been piqued or not. Every word should be chosen wisely when pitching your idea. However, no other part of the pitch has as much potential to invite the listener in as the action of the protagonist. What are we going to see the character actually do in the story? It can be highly tempting to use verbs that describe an inner process as opposed to ones that speak to the visuals we will *see* in our loglines. Any time we mention that a protagonist *realizes*, *learns*, or *recognizes* something in our pitch, a red flag should go up if we are working in a visual medium. These are all actions that happen *inside* the character's psyche and must be accompanied by external actions if we are to know these processes have taken place. Here are eight power verbs that will strengthen your story's pitch or logline and leave little doubt in the mind of your audience that the character is actually going to accomplish something over the course of the narrative.

CHOOSE

Forcing a protagonist to choose between two equally compelling or less than compelling options is a sure way to bring significant conflict to that character's world. These sorts of decisions are universal, and we all relate to being in such situations. In *Thank You For Your Service*, war veteran Adam Schumann must decide between getting the help he needs immediately or instead letting a friend, who might need it worse, take his place.

BUILD

An old politician named Sam Rayburn once said that any jackass can kick down a barn, but it takes a carpenter to build one. When a protagonist is tasked with building something, it speaks to the quality of who she or he is. It tells us that that character comes with qualifications and that other characters must trust that person. Ray Kinsella is tasked with building a baseball stadium in *Field of Dreams*. The goal of creating this magical space is enough to powerfully drive the entire journey of all the characters involved.

CONQUER

One of the oldest actions to occur in storytelling happens when one group of characters tries to overcome another. This archetypal pattern is the basis for most military and sports films, as well as stories that involve one class of people attempting to win something from another. *Kingsman: The Golden Circle* has the protagonistic Kingsman joining forces with an allied spy organization in the United States to conquer a common enemy.

ESCAPE

Another ancient model for crafting a narrative is based around an individual or group that must escape another. Sometimes the scale of the escape is large, as with soldiers who must make it to the border of a dangerous territory. Other times, the scale is personal, as with a lover who must escape their abusive partner. In *Panic Room*, Meg Altman and her daughter must escape from their own home when three men break in looking for a missing fortune.

CAPTURE

As with an escape, the scale of a capture varies as well. A protagonist may be tasked with capturing a villain on the run or simply the heart of another character. When what must be captured is an object, it often must be found first – leaving the capture to occur in the third act. When the capture involves a person, the goal may be accomplished sooner, allowing us to observe the ramifications of the capture afterwards. In *Pirates of the Caribbean: Dead Men Tell No Tales*, Captain Jack Sparrow must capture the trident of Poseidon while on the run from the ghost of another pirate.

SOLVE

While the entire mystery genre is built around this action, *what* must be solved varies from story to story and even expands beyond the realms of this genre. Sometimes what must be examined is the past in order to make sense of the present. Other times, the plot of a story involves getting to the bottom of who another character *is*. In *Mindhunter*, two FBI agents attempt to solve the mystery behind what causes serial killers to commit their monstrous acts.

PREVENT

Many of the most impactful stories are not about a protagonist accomplishing something at all, but rather stopping another character from accomplishing something. These types of narratives are most effective when a deadline is in play, motivating the protagonist to prevent the antagonist's actions before they cause damage to innocent characters. *Shameless* usually revolved around protagonist Fiona Gallagher trying to prevent the destruction of her family from forces both within and outside the house.

SAVE

While often a protagonist may be tasked with saving a tradition, a building, or a relationship, audiences can rarely resist a narrative that involves saving another person – even if that person is the protagonist herself. *The Mountain Between Us* takes a unique spin on this classic story by combining two characters into a situation where they must save themselves *and* each other, as their environment becomes more treacherous, and their relationship grows.

PITCHING 3

POWER ADJECTIVES TO STRENGTHEN YOUR PITCH OR LOGLINE

As storytellers, words are what make or break us. Our ability to flex a wide vocabulary without alienating an audience can mean the difference between a pitch that opens doors for us and one that lacks anything memorable. While it is usually *how* we arrange words that determines the strength of our style, having strong words to arrange is a necessary part of the equation. Adjectives can be an area where storytellers take short cuts. However, these descriptors can make all the difference when trying to convey the qualities of a character, the intensity of a situation, or the desirability of an external goal. *Deafening* is more emotionally expressive than *very noisy*. *Excruciating* affects a reader differently than *extremely painful*. Even an adjective such as *fearless* conjures up a different image than a similar word such as brave. Here are a few power adjectives to consider using when describing the characters, goals, and scenarios in your pitch or log line.

INSTINCTIVE

The word *instinctive* describes a character's ability to trust their own gut. It suggests that a character may be quite independent and even sometimes operate outside of given expectations. We only learn about the instinctive nature of a character when we see those instincts relied on in difficult situations. If we describe a character as *instinctive* in a log line or pitch, we infer that the character has been up against challenging circumstances before. The fate of Western Europe hangs on a single decision by the *instinctive*, newly-elected Prime Minister, Winston Churchill, in *Darkest Hour*.

HORRIFYING

Horrifying has many uses as a descriptor. While it can suggest something that is truly horrific, such as the death of a child. It can also suggest something comedic, such as accidental nudity. It may also be modified to describe another adjective when suggesting, for instance, a character is horrifyingly unaware. In HBO's *Crashing*, a New York comic is forced to make a new start after walking in on his wife in a *horrifying* sexual encounter with one of her co-workers.

DESTITUTE

Destitution occurs in matters of degrees. It can refer to an individual or a situation. While it can simply describe someone who is poor, it often is used to express an extreme situation. It suggests a lack of options, which creates the type of conflict most desired in storytelling. A *destitute* salesman takes custody of his son and struggles to build a new life for both of them while homeless in *The Pursuit of Happyness*.

ULTIMATE

In one story, a protagonist might be described as the *ultimate* bad girl. In another, -- the *ultimate* playboy. In still other stories, the character might search after the *ultimate* artifact of antiquity. The word *ultimate* suggest that a person or item is uncommon, unusual, and to be taken note of. These are the ideas, of course, we build stories around. In *The Handmaid's Tale*, a woman is forced to live under the *ultimate* theocratic dictatorship.

DASHING

Historically, the word *dashing* has been used as a masculine descriptor, though the word has been freed from such patriarchy and is now used to describe the charm or charisma of any character. The words *dazzling* and *enchanting* have been similarly used in feminine contexts but also can be used without concerns for gender identity, and may be more appropriate than *dashing* in the context of your pitch. In *The Marvelous Mrs. Maisel*, the *dashing* Madge is pushed from her comfort zone as a 1950s mother and housewife into the burgeoning New York stand-up comedy scene.

PLUCKY

When a character has shown courage in the face of difficulties, we describe her as *plucky*. The adjective suggests a certain independence and even quirkiness about the character it describes. It paints the picture of someone who cares less about what is thought of them than being true to themselves. In *Lady Bird*, a plucky seventeen-year-old girl overcomes her suffocating environment in order to fully be herself.

SHREWD

The word *shrewd* sometimes calls to mind the image of a businessperson who is more concerned with capitalistic motivations than anything else. However, the word actually refers to someone's keen powers of judgement – their ability to be astute. A shopper can be just as *shrewd* as a merchant. In *The Florida Project*, a *shrewd* hotel manager bonds with tenants while trying to keep their problematic behavior at bay.

PITCHING 4

POWER VERBS THAT WILL STRENGTHEN YOUR PITCH

Many storytellers begin with an internal process or journey as the core of their story. While countless narratives originate with feelings, philosophical beliefs, and experiences in life where we have learned something, eventually those concepts must be externalized if you are working in the realm of visual stories. 'Power verbs' assure the execution of a character's internal journey. They provide insights into what we will see the protagonist actually *do*. They also stir interest in the mind of the listener hearing the pitch and invite their curiosity. Here are several 'power verbs' to bolster your pitch from being weak and toothless to enchanting and captivating.

DELIVERS

Bringing an object, a person, or information to people that need it requires the *delivery* of those things, usually against great odds and conflict. In *The Post*, Meryl Streep and Tom Hanks *deliver* government secrets to the public in the name of holding powerful individuals accountable for questionable actions. The *delivering* of the secrets represents the entire external goal of our protagonists.

EXTRACTS

Extracting something or someone from a difficult environment or circumstances can be a richer way of saying a protagonist is *rescuing* something or someone. In *The Shape of Water*, Sally Hawkins *extracts* the amphibian man from the lab of his captors. *Extraction* suggests the necessity of the *time* it takes to rescue someone. Where a rescue may be quick and sloppy, *extraction* requires precision and accuracy.

LAUNCHES

Simply *beginning* a process lacks the urgency that the word *launch* suggests. Frances McDormand *launches* a campaign that becomes a personal revolution in *Three Billboards Outside Ebbing, Missouri*. *Launching* something indicates a sense of speed and motion. It can be powerful when associated with a character's actions.

MOBILIZES

Assembling a team or a plan can be a tedious process. However, when a protagonist *mobilizes* a group or series of ideas, we imagine military-like actions on the part of the character. Hugh Jackman *mobilizes* a team of people that have been made to feel lesser in their society to create something powerful in *The Greatest Showman*.

NAVIGATES

Stories where the protagonist is a victim of circumstances or constantly faced with challenges that *happen to them* can be difficult and sometimes disengaging for audiences. We connect with characters that have agency. Jessica Chastain *navigates* the legal system, while keeping the gambling underworld at bay in *Molly's Game*. *Navigation* suggest a sense of complication as a character moves through the narrative, efficiently communicating action and opening up the imagination.

DEFEATS

Some of the oldest tales involve a character *winning* a battle of some sort. When a character does win a skirmish, using the verb *defeat* does two things. First, it suggests a more powerful victory rather than just inching out a win. Second, it invites a mention of *who* was defeated – the antagonistic force. Chadwick Boseman *defeats* a savvy legal prosecutor and the unjust system he represents in *Marshall.*

PERSUADES

Persuasion can be tricky in a narrative, as it's a process that takes place in someone's mind. However, *persuading* someone can also be an external action that requires active participation on the part of the protagonist. Jacob Tremblay *persuades* children to see him for who he really is in *Wonder. Persuading* often involves the use of dialogue. However, storytellers should be cautious not to rely too heavily on words when actions can communicate more effectively.

PROCURES

Rescuing someone or something can be a powerful action in a story. The word *rescue* indicates a sense of action, which may be wonderful if that fits the story you are telling. However, if the rescue requires patient calculations and waiting, the verb *procure* may be more accurate and fitting. Michelle Williams *procures* her son from kidnappers in *All the Money in the World.* Using language that most efficiently and mightily communicates the visual storytelling in your narrative will hook the eyes of those that read and the ears of those that hear your pitch.

PITCHING 5

IDEAS TO REMEMBER WHEN PITCHING

When your story is finally completed, you need to be ready to pitch your story to someone that is not legally obligated to tell you they like it. It can be a shock to the system when the story that you mother has claimed is the greatest ever told doesn't hold the attention of the listener you had hoped you would be so captivated. Pitching a story is its own artform. Even the most finely crafted story can be poorly pitched and fail to gain any interest. So how do you communicate the essence of your story without misleading the listener or painting a picture of every scene you've written? Here are a few things to remember when pitching your story.

DON'T KEEP WRITING YOUR STORY WHILE PITCHING

It's not uncommon for brilliance to strike while pitching your story. More than one storyteller has had a great idea in the middle of describing their story to someone else. It can be tempting to incorporate the idea on the fly, veering off track from the story you have available to send someone who might be interested. Without fail, you will be immediately asked to send it over and have to fess up or make drastic surgery to your story in a panicked rush. Save yourself the trouble and DO NOT pitch something you have not already executed.

PRACTICE, PRACTICE, PRACTICE

Looking like you are effortlessly pitching a story without any forethought and actually being able to do it are two WILDLY different skillsets. Most casual pitches that seem off the cuff are actually rehearsed to no end in order to appear that way. Don't rely on your improv skills if you know you are going to have the opportunity to present your story to someone who may be interested. Practice until you know your pitch backwards and forwards and STICK TO IT once you get your opportunity.

KEEP IT SHORT AND AIMED AT PROVOKING QUESTIONS

One of the most common mistakes newbies make when pitching their material is telling their listener FAR too much about their story. Skilled storytellers share just enough to arouse curiosity but not so much the listener becomes bored. This can be a tough balance to strike when you are starting out. Your goal should be to get the listener to engage in your story so deeply that they begin imagining it and asking questions that will help them paint the image they are crafting in their mind. Create a 5-minute version of your pitch, a 2-minute version, a sixty second version, and even a one sentence pitch. The key is to hone these versions of your short pitch in a way that gains you the opportunity to offer a longer version of the story later.

KNOW THE GENRE AND/OR FAMILY OF FILMS YOURS BELONGS IN

It's jaw dropping how many storytellers complete a feature-length story without ever thinking about where their story fits in the larger family of narratives that a listener is already familiar with. Telling someone right away what genre or family of stories yours belongs in gives the listener handles that they will desperately need in order to engage. Remember, while you have spent hours and hours in the world of your story and thoroughly understand its nuances, the person you are pitching to is coming to your pitch with a blank slate. They literally know NOTHING. Anything you can offer to orient them in your story will help them begin to engage in your pitch and avoid confusion.

RELAX

Nerves have robbed more storytellers of a successful pitch than any other single factor. Letting nerves cause you to speak too quickly, become flustered, or cause you to forget your own material are all experiences that other storytellers have fallen victim to. Relax. Take three deep breaths before you pitch. Make eye contact. Speak slowly but not unnaturally. Smile and enjoy the reward of getting to share the fruits of your labor with someone else.

www.ingramcontent.com/pod-product-compliance
Lightning Source LLC
Chambersburg PA
CBHW021138090426
42740CB00008B/838